Pound Wise

Parenting

Creative parenting on a budget

Ruth Wise

First edition printed and published in the United Kingdom 2023.

A CIP catalogue record of this book is available from the British Library.

ISBN: 979-8-3936815-4-8 (Paperback)
Imprint: Independently published
Typesetting: Matthew J Bird

For further information about this book, please contact the author at:
Email: ruth@ruthwise.uk or
Facebook: Poundwise Parenting
Website   www.ruthwise.uk

This book is dedicated to every parent

Contents

Introduction

I'm glad you are here

I am so happy that you are reading this book, as you have joined a worldwide group of parents and caregivers trying to be the best they can be, in whatever circumstances.

I aim to inspire and encourage anyone involved in raising children on a limited budget. I am now a grandma, watching the next generation of parents do a fantastic job against incredible odds, and I want to support you.

When you embarked on your parenting journey, you could not have imagined a worldwide pandemic's impact on you or your children. Any other time, you might have turned to the older generation and asked how they coped in similar situations, but there is no precedent of a pandemic in recent memory, and we were as confused and frightened as you.

Be proud of yourself

Be proud because, somehow, you have made it through. You have developed creative skills out of necessity, as you have adapted to constantly changing rules. Many of you found yourselves juggling work and home-schooling, some lost income, and the majority lost physical contact with wider families and peers. It was a tough time, but you got through it.

Just as you thought you had emerged, and life was returning to normal, you are now forced to cope with a massive cost-of-living crisis. Your children still need parenting but you have less money than you anticipated. You are now having to think about how you spend every single pound.

Use this book as a springboard

Let it help you develop your creative skills and make unforgettable memories with your children, that you might not have had if you weren't on a low budget.

Turn a negative into a positive.

You were not born with the ability to think creatively; it is a skill you develop. Instead of seeing the lack of money as a disaster, you can change how you think and welcome it as a chance to become more creative.

My website www.ruthwise.uk is a vital resource

This book is full of suggestions and ideas, but it will only succeed if you think collaboratively. The free website supporting this book is brimming with links to a world full of creative people, so you can use their ideas and suggest some of your own. The Covid pandemic left a positive legacy of many online support groups, a significantly increased use of online meetings, and a greater willingness to work with each other to get through. We must use these to overcome the challenge of having less money.

What this book is not about

I am not telling you how to bring up your child. Nor is this book concerned with the right or wrong way of doing anything. Your children may be difficult, frustrating and ungrateful, whatever you try. More money or anything you read, will not change that.

You may have to wait to be appreciated

Some ideas will work like a charm once and be disastrous another time. Other ideas will not work for, you but there will be ideas that will give you a creative and accessible way of doing something.

It will require effort, so do not expect a quick rush of gratitude. Your child will be clueless about how much work you are putting into raising them for at least another forty years, so get over it. It wasn't until my husband was forty, with six children of his own, that he wrote a thankyou letter to his parents about what he finally appreciated.

A more creative approach can be beneficial even if you have money

This isn't only about making it through when you are short of money. It is for parents who want to enrich their children by trying new ideas and spending more time with them.

Don't panic. It is impossible to do all the ideas you simply have to survive the parenting experience.

I tried everything in the book except wild swimming

I raised six children on a meagre budget but it never occurred to me that it was a problem. Since we chose to have a large family, I had to be creative to make it through and ensure that the children didn't miss out.

This book has been written from well-tried and tested experiences and offers you glimpses into our budget-parenting journey. We all have different circumstances to deal with in life, so I hope that the variety of ideas presents a path for each reader.

You alone know what will work for you and your family so I hope you enjoy reading this book, which has more ideas than you will know what to do with, and move from a low budget situation to a creative mindset solution.

CHANGE
YOUR MIND

1

Change your thinking if you can't change your budget

There are times in life when you can feel trapped by your circumstances. You may have tried everything possible to increase your income and reduce expenditure. The children have not cut back on their needs or wants, and you only have this precious chance to bring them up as best as you can.

You cannot change the budget or the children. There is only one thing that you have any power to change, and that is the way you think about your situation.

Changing your attitude is the only way out of your circumstantial trap.

Be proud of yourself and confident in your ability

Firstly, be proud of how far you have come and how well you have survived.

Secondly, be confident that you can turn your situation around.

Don't be overwhelmed by the huge online pressure to be 'better parents'. I know first-hand that you aren't going to get it all right. You can only do your best.

My book will give you ways to turn the lack of money into a positive thing and ensure your children don't think they are lacking.

Choose your words wisely around your children

Many parents today are experiencing significant hardship and facing unimaginable challenges. They spend a lot of time discussing gas and electricity bills. Shopping has become a chore and feeding children a healthy diet is becoming increasingly complex with the rising prices.

Listen to your dialogue with other adults, and be aware of what your children hear.

These conversations need to be adult-only since children pick up on more than we anticipate and such conversations may make them feel anxious. Let them know that there is less money so they can understand your decisions and appreciate what they have, but don't burden them.

When they are adults, they will understand much better how amazing you are, but they probably aren't going to thank you now.

It is hard to parent with less money, but it is not impossible. Remember that it's your problem, not your children's.

The solution is that we need to work together

We need to approach the situation positively and united. We can turn it around and become better parents and give our children a legacy of creativity and positivity that they wouldn't have had if we'd had more money.

That might sound like an impossible dream but, as you read each chapter of this book, you will discover a lot you can do to make life better. Not everything will be a quick win but you are already on the journey.

Use what you learned in the pandemic to get you through the economic downturn

Although the Covid pandemic was challenging for many people, positive aspects can be salvaged as we learned skills which are helpful for budgeting.

Many parents were forced to spend a lengthy time at home with their children, with little money.

The internet became a source of inspiration and communication, and creativity flourished. Zoom became a norm. We had to learn to adapt to a different lifestyle and, somehow, we all managed to change.

It wasn't all negative. People discovered latent skills and many positively engaged with society and wanted to help others through the situation.

We now have many online resources and ways of communicating, which give us the foundation for working together to help each other with tight budgets.

The good news is that we have the resources

The advantage of not having the internet when I was raising children was less international pressure to be perfect parents. However, we were disadvantaged by not having the fantastic online resources which are available now.

We had a lot of books, although little time to read, and each other. Now, you can search instantly for resources to get new ideas. You can watch a video to learn a new skill. You can communicate across the world to find creative ideas and encouragement.

You are part of the solution

Let this book be your springboard. The time you have raising children is relatively short, although it feels endless while you are doing it. From my standpoint now, it went too fast. Trust me, you haven't got time to waste by regretting that you have less money than you thought you would have. You have to get on and make the most of your parenting journey. Use this book to plan how you are going to do that.

Give your children a positive legacy

When we speak to older people about their experiences of significant adversity, such as war, there are two possible versions of their narrative. They could have given us a legacy whereby we feel we don't have enough, but they gave us one of hope. They talk about coming together, sharing, opening homes, having empathy and building together.

We can learn so much from the older generation. At the time, they must have experienced horrendous fear yet, somehow, they haven't passed that on. The legacy we want for our children is to make the best of a situation, rather than them thinking they don't have enough.

This is all about building positive memories and doing incredible things with few resources.

Your situation is unique

Your parenting story will not be the same as anyone else's. It can be hard not to compare yourself with others, but it rarely leads to a positive outcome.

Some parts of this book will apply to everyone, but some may not apply to your situation, so feel free to skip those parts. I won't be offended. To be honest, we do not have time to waste. Embrace the ideas that work for you.

You are amazing and we need you.

In my experience, many people don't recognise their creativity, but it is a matter of perspective. Any parent knows that, to get through a day in one piece with their child takes more creativity than Michelangelo showed in his lifetime.

I hope this book will affirm what you are already doing, spark new ideas and encourage you to share your creativity. A revolution will happen when we come together in a common challenge and find a shared solution.

One of my greatest joys in writing this book has been to hear the amazing ideas of other parents who are facing the same challenges.

As you journey through this book and have an idea, I encourage you to never assume that it is not worth sharing, as it may be a great idea for someone else in a similar situation.

The free Poundwise Parenting website, www.ruthwise.uk offers a range of updated ideas, as well as a forum for you to input your suggestions.

Put the fun back into dysfunctional

Families come in all shapes, sizes and colours. We must focus on our similarities, not on our differences. We are united by a lack of money and the desire to be better parents.

I have discovered that, for one reason or another, most families are dysfunctional. This book is my attempt to put the fun back into dysfunctional, without spending too much.

This book has great ideas even if you do have money

Maybe you are not struggling financially, but just want to be more creative in your parenting. You want to raise their children to understand the value of money and don't want them to expect expensive outings and possessions.

This book is for you too.

2

Develop your creativity

Develop your creative mind

The Oxford Languages definition of creativity is: *the use of imagination or original ideas to create something.*

Being creative is not something you already are or are not — it is a skill you can develop

The power to change your actions is within you. It is an exciting thought that our underused brains can be developed more by having less money. If we become more creative, so will our children, and we are giving them a positive gift that will continue through future generations.

Let a melon change your thinking

You decide to serve melon and these are your options:

1. Go to an expensive supermarket and buy ready-wrapped and ready-cut honeydew melon; cubed - at least £8 for 6 portions.

2. Go to a less expensive supermarket and buy ready-wrapped melon slices which you can cut smaller — about £6.

3. Go to a shop with melons on offer which you can cut into slices - about £1.70.

A poundwise parent would choose option 3 and get at least two hours of purposeful activity by using the melon in some of the following activities.

- Cut the melon into slices, then cut along the top to form cubes and arrange these in an interesting shape. Stick a straw or cocktail stick in the top, make a paper triangle, and you have a boat. Using cocktail sticks and paper only, who can make the best Viking ship? You can eat it after the competition.

- The melon seeds can be dried and painted, then threaded into jewellery or glued to make a picture.

- The melon's skin can be used in a contest to make the most interesting or scary eye mask by cutting holes in it. I wouldn't recommend you put the skins too close to the face. You can judge just by looking at them.

- Who can make the best shadow? Cut out shapes from the melon skin to make interesting shadows when held in front of a torch or candle in a dark room.

You see, it isn't about having only £1.70 to buy a dessert for six. It is how you go about it. Depending on the age of your children, you can discuss how to make a melon more interesting and encourage their ideas. By doing this, you develop their creativity and you will be amazed at their brilliant ideas.

Stop yearning for a life with spare money

Embrace the idea that, whilst there can be a lot of pressure for children to have the newest technology or the latest fashion, for most of us, our fondest memories are not based on these things.

Don't worry if you don't have brilliant ideas. If you are motivated, you can find lots of good ideas with helpful videos on the internet. Just type "Creative activities for children" into a search engine and you will be inundated with suggestions. There are many online groups of like-minded parents. It is time to link up with them and try some of their suggestions.

BUILD YOUR RESOURCES

3

What have you got that is free?

What have you already got?

It is time to take a look around you. Instead of thinking about what you would like from shops and websites, look at the vast resources you already have and consider how they can be used more.

The following chapters will unpack some practical actions but a change of heart is needed first.

Here are some ideas to start with.

Walking

If you can't afford to go to different places, walk with your children and invent games to make it interesting.

- Go for walks to meet and interact with people, even if only by smiling and saying, "Hello". You never know what they may be struggling with, and you could make them feel special.

- Count how many people smile or say "Hello".

- Use online scavenger hunt lists to make your walk more interesting.

- Don't just stay in your area, travel somewhere else and explore online guided walks.

Singing

If you can breathe, you can sing. It doesn't matter if you are in tune. Put some music on and pretend it's a karaoke session. You might even discover a latent talent.

- A fun game is to turn the music down and continue singing. When you turn the sound up, see if anyone is still in tune and can join back in.

Clapping and drumming

Encourage your children to add rhythm to music.

- Try clapping on the offbeat and attempt different rhythms.

- Turn saucepans upside down for an impromptu drum set.

- Blast out music and sing along, adding rhythm with wooden spoons.

Remember, this is all free.

Family games

There are lots of radio programmes to pinch ideas from and turn into a free family game.

- Make your own version of "Desert Island Discs". Let the children choose their favourite piece of music and say why they like it. Or ask them if a piece of music prompts a memory.

- Play "Just a minute" and see how long your children can talk about a subject without hesitation, deviation or repetition.

- Do your version of a quiz game your family likes. You only need a chair and a bright light, and you can play "Who wants to be a Millionaire?" Go online for questions to ask and you can download the theme music to add authenticity to the game.

- Another great game is "Would you rather?" Everyone chooses two options and then asks someone else which one they prefer. It doesn't sound exciting but try these five and you'll see it can be fun and an excellent way for children to talk about feelings and choices. Search online for "Would you Rather - questions for kids". Make sure you add "for kids" as there are some grim choices for adults.

Would you rather slide down rainbows or jump on clouds?

Would you rather eat a dead bug or a live worm?

Would you rather have a booming voice or a whisper?

Would you rather be 2 years older or 5 years younger?

Would you rather have crab-claw hands or wheels for feet?

Dancing

If you can move, you can dance. No one is watching and children usually love to dance. It can be therapeutic. When I was stressed with the children, or when they argued, putting on music and dancing or singing considerably defused the situation.

- A fun activity is to allow one child to be the leader and the rest have to copy their actions, so then it doesn't matter if you can't dance.

- If you want to take it to a more serious level, there are hundreds of YouTube videos to learn new styles of dance steps as a family.

You can relax together if you have music and can move your body. At a simple level, lie on the floor with your children, then ask them to close their eyes while music plays. Talk about what each person can see and how they are feeling. You are doing something special together and it is entirely free.

Perhaps my next book should be, "The Bluffers' Guide to Parenting".

Keep Fit

You can also establish your keep-fit sessions, adapted for the age of the children. Build up a set of exercises they enjoy but be mindful of warming up and cooling down, as it can be easy to overdo it.

My Experience

I confess that once I was given a class of thirty stroppy fourteen years olds and was told I had to do Keep Fit with them. I didn't have a clue, so I kept them going non-stop for the whole time. I didn't know anything about warming up or stretching then. In the following days, you could see which children had been in my class, as none of them could walk properly.

One of the good products from the pandemic is the quantity of YouTube keep-fit videos. However, don't be limited by them as you can work out your own moves. Maybe your children can lead the session and you do whatever they say. It is all positive and team building.

It is always worth looking in your local area for an athletic centre or park area nearby, where your children could set up races and outdoor activities.

Wild/outdoor swimming

This is not something I was able to do with my children, but it has become popular. It is free, so cheaper than going to a swimming pool. There is now an Outdoor Swimming Society website that offers safety advice, as well as locations of swim maps to take your children to.

How can you maximise your toys and activities?

Now is the time to look at everything in your house and see if you can add play value to it. The aim is to cut down on waste and find free resources. Seeing how productive you can make an item can be challenging but you must use every item and opportunity if you are on a budget.

Considering play value is a helpful way to look at toys you buy or already possess. If a toy has only one purpose, it is costly and quickly discarded. Conversely, bricks have a high play value.

Consider how many things you can do with a toy. Go through them and sort out which are worth keeping. Prioritise the most valuable toys if you are on a budget or have limited space.

My Experience

I learned this lesson when we swapped houses with a Dutch family. Our house was full of boxed toys and we spent ages sorting them before we left.

Their family also had six children and we expected them to have a similar set of toys for our children to play with.

We were shocked to discover that the only toys they had were several boxes of Lego and a bike each. As the cycling system in Holland is excellent, our children became more physically active. They learned to adapt, still playing endlessly, and were much more creative with fewer games.

4

Art box

Why do you need an art box?

Children need to be able to create and express themselves, and there are many resources available to explore the benefits and wonder of art. From a budget point of view, once you have the basics, it is a very cheap activity.

It is not necessary to buy an expensive art box that contains perfectly-arranged crayons, pencils and paints. You don't need a neat container. Instead, you would benefit from a larger, less tidy and more creative art box.

I have used the plastic crate type as they are easy to clean and manoeuvre, although it is ecologically preferable to use a large cardboard box.

An added benefit to creating your own art box is that your children can decorate it, which provides another free activity.

Make sure it is tall enough to take upright paint and glue bottles. Trust me, you will not get through parenting without a lid being left off, and you could lose a whole bottle if it is stored on its side. Although it requires an initial investment, it is cheaper in the long term to buy large bottles of ready-made paint. If you buy them individually, you will need black, white, blue, yellow and red, as you can make all the other colours from these. Most online shops sell economy packs of 6 or 8.

Having an art box saves a lot of time, as all the resources are in one place and children do not spend ages rummaging through drawers and cupboards to find them.

If your children have a wide age range, it is safer to have a separate box for the younger ones, with only plastic scissors and no glue.

How you fill this box will change depending on the ages of your children. I suggest that there are a few basic requirements, most of which can be purchased from pound shops.

What you need in an art box

- **PVA Glue**

  I haven't found a good glue recipe, so you will need to buy this, preferably in a squeezy bottle, but always check that it is washable. Don't waste money on tiny pots as the larger ones are usually better value.

- **Scissors: short and long-bladed**

  Get the sort which is age-appropriate for your children. Younger children can have plastic ones but make sure they work, as you don't want to be asked to cut everything.

- **Paper**

  Collect any packaging that comes into your house of various shades and thicknesses.

- **Paper clips**

- **Sellotape**

- **Paint brushes**

  Collect a wide variety of brushes, including old toothbrushes.

- **Coloured pencils**

- **Felt tip pens**

- **Glue sticks**
  Buy these if you have the money as they can be expensive, but are the most efficient way of not creating a mess. Be careful though, as some of the cheap ones are useless. Make sure the lids are always put back on as they dry quickly and become unusable.

- **Lids of ice cream tubs**
  These are suitable for mixing paint.

- **Yoghurt pots**
  These are useful for decanting glue and holding cold water to clean brushes.

- **Plastic glue spreader**
  These can be made from lids.

Other helpful items to add:

- Stapler and staples

- Pipe cleaners

- Bits of sponge

- Hole puncher

- Chalks

- Powder paints

- Split pins

- Blu Tack

- Cotton buds

- Picture magazines

- Catalogues

Tip:

Keep non-toxic spray and cleaning cloths (see Chapter 18: Keeping the house clean) in the box so that children can clear up after themselves quickly and easily. Stains are more likely to be removed if dealt with immediately.

Make a construction box

Alongside the art box, it may be helpful to collect lots of junk to stimulate the children's imagination. Once it is set up, the children will start adding to it, which is an excellent way to encourage them to recycle.

Suggestions:

- Robust scissors

- Plasticine

- Newspapers

- Craft dough (see Chapter 13: Making a mess on purpose)

- Thick craft paper

- Any recyclable box, pot or object

- Masking tape

- Thicker tape (insulating tape, etc)

- Cutting board (perhaps an old chopping board)

- Scraps of felt, string, cotton, embroidery silks, wool, etc

- Paper roll tubes

- Straws

- Packing materials (foam, bubble wrap)

- Egg boxes

- Cocktail sticks

5

Dressing-up box

Make a dressing-up box

This is one of the cheapest toys but is one that children will probably play with the most.

Children in every generation have enjoyed pretending to be grown-up or being someone else. It seems inherent in every child to attempt to walk in high heels or plod around in their parents' slippers.

Why should we encourage dressing up?

- Pretending is an important part of children's development and has a significant fun value.

- It develops language skills by extending vocabulary and communication.

- The interaction develops interpersonal skills and imagination.

- It allows children the opportunity to be someone else and explore emotions in a safe setting.

- You will be surprised by what you learn about your child by watching them dress up.

Dressing-up boxes are a fantastic resource all year round and, if you haven't already got one, it is a good idea to start building one. You will need to have a wide range of clothes and accessories to stimulate your children's imaginations and possibly yours.

How do you source a dressing-up box?

Look through your cupboards and ask your wider family and friends. You will be amazed at what you can collect. Many people hold on to clothes and accessories that they will never wear again but don't know what to do with. Although children like them, I would never suggest buying ready-made dressing-up clothes. You can often find them in boot sales, jumble sales, and charity shops, as well as Freecycle sites.

What can go in a dressing-up box?

You can put anything in a dressing-up box but the following list, although not exhaustive, should give you some ideas.

- Hats
- Coats and jackets
- Dresses
- Trousers
- Large T-shirts
- Belts
- Gloves
- Shoes
- Handbags
- Jewellery
- Feathers
- Hair ties
- Scarves
- Glasses and sunglasses

Access to a mirror is helpful as children find it fun to see their images when putting on different clothes and accessories.

Keep it fresh

The box's contents will change according to the ages and stages of your children. Some items will be used endlessly, and others rarely, so you can repeatedly eliminate anything they outgrow or never use. Keep adding to the collection and don't forget to wash the clothes, especially if they spend half the summer being worn in the garden.

You could have two sets of dressing-up boxes to provide variety and be available, depending on the number of children you have.

If it suits your situation, you could have individual box collections of:

- Hats
- Shoes
- Bags
- Accessories
- Dresses

How do you store your dressing-up things?

If you have plenty of space, you may have a cupboard to store all the clothes and keep everything tidy and separate, but it can be a problem if space is tight. I used empty suitcases and put the clothes in bags when we went away and needed the cases.

Don't have rules for playing with the box

Children should be able to access clothes without considering gender. It is a theatrical box and pretend play is the order of the day.

Dressing up should be child-led and they should be free to have ideas about what to do with the clothes. Interestingly, once they dress up, role play follows naturally and leads to hours of exciting activity.

Getting together with friends

If you have like-minded friends, you can have dressing-up box gatherings. Invite each family to bring along a selection from their box to let the children play with. Other people's things always seem more enjoyable and children won't need much encouragement. Another activity which does not cost anything.

My Experience

We always kept dressing-up clothes for our children and I enjoyed finding things to add to them at jumble sales. Out of all the toys, it was used the most but cost the least. I still have some of the clothes in a suitcase because they hold some of my happiest memories of my children growing up. I found that each child had their favourites.

One child loved the swirling skirt and spent most of her time swishing around and making large sweeping gestures.

Another always put on the black cape and turned into a pirate, regardless of what the others were doing, and kept the cloak on all day.

Another child was more bothered about the shoes and clopped about, happily organising everyone else. She took on different roles, depending on which shoes she was wearing. Interestingly, she carried her love of shoes into her adult life.

Putting on plays

Many children want to put on a play when they have dressed up, with one child generally being the director and having all the main parts. These can be dull occasions but stick with them and join in the game.

You may have a role in the play if they want you to although, usually, you must be the audience.

Alternatively, you can make tickets, arrange the room like a theatre, put a cloth across the front of the table if it helps, or do anything to encourage them. You might even have a child who writes scripts. Videoing the plays would produce a lot of fun and beautiful memories.

I often pretended to be the ice cream lady at the theatre and give our children a cone at the end of the play.

Confession

I have watched endless plays and have always clapped enthusiastically and displaying great enjoyment. Some of the plays were very tedious but the children always thought we were a wonderful audience.

Time goes quickly and it won't be long before they become teenagers. They will suddenly stop doing plays with stuff out of the dressing-up box.

Trust me. You will be glad that you seized the moments.

6

Music box

Music as communication

Music is a beautiful and free commodity. My generation had CDs and cassettes, but now the world is awash with fantastic music through the internet. If you can get music into your house, you must use this resource fully.

Listen to each other's music

A great activity is listening to each other's choices as each family member will have a different preference. You can do this informally or let each person choose music to play while eating, for example.

Another idea is to search for an unfamiliar music genre as it is good to encourage children to enjoy and understand different types.

Discuss how music makes you feel. It can evoke memories, so talk about what it reminds you of.

If you have no internet access, you could buy an old CD player (see Chapter 19: Jumble sales and boot sales). CDs are now out of fashion, so can be picked up cheaply.

If you do have internet access, you can make your own playlists. Amazon Music is a fantastic app for this and, with help, children can make their own. They can have one for homework time, one for relaxing, one for the bath, etc. Creating the lists is exciting and it means you can quickly access the music you like, when you want it.

If your children are ahead of you on this, and they often are, get them to make playlists for you. At least for a short time, they will listen to what you like.

Music can change an atmosphere. When playing what you enjoy, chores seem more manageable. Have a 'clean my room' playlist for the children, so that they aim to have it finished by the end of the songs. You can be as creative as you like.

Music for dancing

You can find music with great rhythm and put it on loudly so that everyone dances, wherever they are in the house.

You can have a dance session with the music each one has chosen. If you want to learn to dance, there is a proliferation of people teaching dance steps of every genre on YouTube.

If you don't like dancing, you can always do the Conga. Nominate a leader, hold on to their waist and start going around the house in time to the music.

It doesn't matter if no one knows what to do. Music is a beautiful way to communicate with each other.

Make a music box

We have always had a music box containing instruments which I accrued from jumble sales, such as small drums, tambourines and maracas. We added homemade instruments, such as containers with beads to shake.

Learn to play an instrument

It would be great if you could afford to send your children to private lessons to learn to play an instrument. If the budget does not allow that, you need to find alternatives.

Perhaps find a friend who can play an instrument and will give your child lessons. Alternatively, YouTube can offer online lessons.

Many apps can make learning possible and you can download piano keyboards on a tablet or touchscreen computer.

Second-hand instruments may be available online or in a jumble sale, or you might be able to borrow one.

Make your own instruments

Once you start thinking about musical instruments, you will be amazed at how many ideas you can come up with.

- Fill a container with small objects (such as screws) and, as long as you can secure it with a lid, you have a maraca.

- Stretch elastic bands across an ice cream tub and you will make some excellent sounds.

- Put rubber sheeting across a saucepan with a tight elastic band and you have made a drum.

- Even at a basic level, an upside-down saucepan can be drummed with a wooden spoon.

- Put a cork in one end of a hollow wooden tube. Fill it with dried rice grains, cork the other end and you have made a rain stick.

- Any stick can be used as a rhythm stick. The cheapest one is probably a wooden spoon.

- An exciting activity is to arrange glasses or bottles of various sizes and put water in them, then strike the side with a spoon and listen to the tone. It is possible to arrange them in order and make a rough xylophone.

I found it helpful to always have instruments available so that the children could join in whenever they heard music in the house.

Enjoy musical skills

Some of your family may be able to play an instrument. If this is the case, encourage them to play as much as possible for the family. You can support them with your homemade instruments. Many children struggle to practise but if you can encourage them in any way, it is all free music.

Could you set up a show and record it?

It would be fun to record the children playing different instruments or singing. Set up a talent show or music concert. Remember, this is not for anyone else, just your own family.

Karaoke

You could do an impromptu karaoke session and you don't need a real microphone. Play any music and let the children pretend to be the singer. Various apps can convert your phone or computer into a karaoke machine. Be careful though, as some require a subscription. Some YouTube videos mean you can get close to the effect.

Games with music

There are many different games you can play with music.

Musical statues

Play the music and stop it at any time. The family members have to hold their pose and not move. As soon as they move, they are out of the game and the rest of you keep going until there is one person left.

Or you can play a simple version where children hold their position until the music restarts.

Drawing to Music

Give the children a large piece of paper, crayons, pencils, felt pens and paint. Put on music and get them to express what they hear in their drawing. This is a fascinating exercise.

A couple of children could work on the same piece of paper and draw collaboratively. The end result is not important, but it encourages children to listen to music and express their ideas visually.

It is also fun to try this activity as a family, by putting a large sheet of paper on a table and everyone drawing on it together. It can work well if you move around the table each time you have a different piece of music.

What is the song?

Clap out a song without singing it, and see if the children can work out the tune. It is a brilliant way to teach listening skills and children are surprisingly good at it.

Get them to clap out a tune for you.

Dance like an animal

Put on music and let the children pretend to be animals dancing. You can call out the animal's name, and then keep changing it. If you have any picture books, you can show the relevant picture.

My Experience

I struggled with depression when my children were young but found that music was often a lifeline. Sometimes when they were driving me crazy, I would declare a "music session". I played the piano, albeit poorly, put out the music box and they would play instruments, dance and jump around like crazy until I stopped playing.

It worked exceptionally well for us all.

Limbo Game

Put a rope or scarf across two pieces of furniture and let the children lean backwards to go under it, with their feet first. This game works better with music. Keep lowering the rope until the last one can't get under it.

STAYING-IN
ACTIVITIES

7

Containers

You would be amazed how many containers and packages come into your house. It is time to make use of each one and convert it into a valuable play resource. Never throw a container away again. They all have free-play potential.

Which ice cream containers are best?

This next section does not work with the cardboard packaging of up-market ice creams. This is good news as, the chances are, you can't afford them anyway.

Aim to find the cheapest ice cream in the most useful container. Ideally, we should not be using plastic but, if you have some, make sure you get a lot of use out of them. The basic rules are: never throw one away and get everyone to save them for you. Each size is useful for different things.

You can find endless ideas online for how to use containers, so I will only include a few of my favourites in this book.

Go to my Poundwise Parenting website for links to other ideas and add yours there.

Miniature gardens

One idea is to convert the container into a miniature garden. Your children will come up with the most creative ideas. The goal is not to get a garden where anything grows but to use bits from your garden to make a mini garden on the base of the container. Some very clever gardens can be made using stones, earth, flowers, leaves and grass. I must admit I cheated and used a circle of aluminium foil to make a pond in some of mine.

These gardens look good on the windowsill for about a week and then you can throw it all back into the garden. Make sure you keep the plastic container.

Potion pots

As a child, I used to be fascinated with potions. My children used to play a game called "Making potions" where possibilities were endless and all kinds of brews were created.

Fill an ice cream container with petals and, as it mulches down, an evil concoction is created, which we used to call 'perfume'. If you haven't got a garden, gather petals that have fallen in the park.

It's a great challenge as even tea dregs can become part of a potential witches' brew. Set out a container at the beginning of the day and see what potions you can create by the evening. If the weather allows, start and finish this game outdoors.

Make up a story around the brew. The end product is unimportant but it provides a rich language activity.

Snail houses

My children often used ice cream containers to make houses for snails. I am not talking about making a good house for a pet snail as you can get that on the internet. This is a time-limited play activity. It is great fun, as garden snails are remarkable to watch. Your children will pick them up anyway, so you might as well make a play event out of it.

The idea is that they create a world for the snail and spend time collecting stones and leaves to make it more interesting. For one day, they can watch the snail and see where it goes. Make sure that there is a moist environment for it.

This is cheaper and less hassle than having a pet, since all the snails are released back into a more natural habitat at the end of the day. Ensure you wash the container out well afterwards.

With lots of children and containers, you could adapt this idea to run your own snail hotel.

On the subject of snails, you can make a snail gymnasium out of things in the garden. The children must wash their hands and, if it bothers you, they can wear plastic gloves but it is nowhere near as much fun.

Cardboard boxes

I have always firmly believed in a cardboard box's creative value. It is best if you do not dictate to the child what it should be used for.

I remember asking my seven-year-old son to throw a box away. He looked hurt and said, "That's not a box; it's a boat."

Boxes are easy to obtain. Some supermarkets store them, and you can usually help yourself. Other times you may need to be more resourceful and ask shops if they would let you have some. It often helps to ask in advance, and they will save them for you. I found shoe shops to be the best source as shoe boxes are perfect for dolls houses and multi-storey car parks.

A few ideas with boxes

Put different sized boxes upside down on the floor. Using wooden spoons they can be converted into a drum set. Play music with a strong rhythm and your child will do the rest. At the end of the day, the boxes are often useless, but who cares? Simply recycle them.

Hide an object in the boxes and put them in different places for the child to hunt. If you are going to have a snack time, this is an excellent chance to hide small bags of raisins, etc. Somehow a box hunt makes it more fun. Don't ask me why.

My children were adept at converting boxes to dolls houses. Either put them sideways so that they become different rooms or, with the base of the box on the floor, put homemade furniture in it. You will be surprised how sophisticated these properties can become.

Boxes can be used to make walls and barriers. Your lounge can become a fortress, your carpet can become a sea for boats, and your garden/patio can be transformed into a village of houses.

Boxes can be painted, have paper stuck on them, or left just as they are. A fun activity is to give each child a large box and see if they can attach leaves (an excellent game in autumn) to camouflage their box, then hide in it.

If you have a large appliance delivered, it is always worthwhile to save the box. They are wonderful for children and can become anything they want, from playhouses to forts and boats. You might need duct tape to strengthen the edges if lots of children are going in and out.

Diorama

A diorama displays an idea three-dimensionally. There are plenty of ideas on the internet with step-by-step guides. In the simplest terms, you put a box (shoe boxes are perfect for this) on its side. Cut a small hole in the top to allow light in.

Choose a theme to decorate the outside of the box. For added effect, use a mixture of paint, craft paper or material. Decorate the inside of the cut-out. You can then mount cardboard cut-out shapes from the bottom or hang them from the top. This will complete your diorama.

You can make anything that your child is interested in but fish tanks, dinosaur landscapes and farms are ideas to start with, if you need inspiration.

Make special boxes

Some children love having their own collection of things that are important to them. Give each child a box and let them decorate the outside with pictures of anything they like, using images from catalogues and magazines. They can put their name on it, using letters they have coloured. The box could be lined with material and anything could be stuck on the outside to make it more interesting.

The most important aspect of this project is that each child is expressing what is important to them. Encourage them to lead the activity, which can go on for ages.

Tin cans

If you are cooking on a budget, you may use tin cans. Do not throw these away. Wash them thoroughly and ensure there are no sharp edges, and then create games with them. The play value of a set of tins is incredibly high and they are free.

- Cover the tins with paper and let the children decorate them. Add a number on the side of each tin to make games more interesting

- Pile the tins in a vertical pyramid and see who can knock the most down with a ball. This is best played outdoors or with a soft ball indoors. It is like an old-fashioned coconut shy.

- Arrange the tins in a horizontal pyramid on the floor, as in a bowling alley, and see how many tins you can knock over by rolling a ball.

- You can do more activities by making holes in the tin cans. The easiest way to do this without a drill is to bang a nail into it with a hammer and then remove the nail. Create a hole in the solid circle end of two tins. Make a large knot in some thick string, thread it through one hole, then put it into the other tin, and add another knot. Make the string taut and use the tins as old-fashioned telephones.

- Use small tins to cook small cakes, perfect for tiny Christmas cakes. It is more fun for children to make individual cakes than a large one.

- Decorate a tin and use it as a pencil holder. Hang it with string to make extra storage by adding four holes.

- Get lots of tins and, with one hole at the end of each, make a wind chime by hanging them close together.

Encourage your children to grow things from seeds in containers. It is a great activity to plant seeds and watch them grow, and exciting if they make something edible. Lettuce is a good example for a high success rate and quick return.

8

Challenges

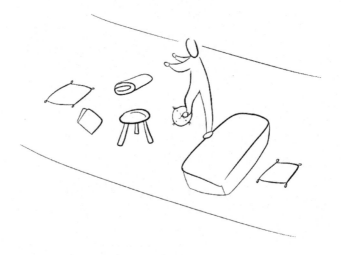

Turn an idea into an event

There are times when you have to create something out of thin air. You can learn to turn anything into an event. Try the following challenges but get your children to come up with their own ideas.

- Can you make a bridge, that will take the weight of a bag of sugar, using only newspaper and sticky tape?

- Can you make a boat that floats, using only one piece of paper?

- Can you get water to move from one corner of the draining board to the other side, using anything you can find in the kitchen? Be warned: this can produce waterfalls and all sorts.

- Can you use cushions and other objects to get from one side of a room to another, without touching the floor?

- Can you spend 20 minutes playing a game, without speaking?

- Can you eat dinner blindfolded?

The £1 or £2 game

This is one of the most enjoyable games you can play when you have a couple of hours in a town with limited funds.

Write each person's name on separate pieces of paper and ask everyone to choose one. You must buy a gift for that person which they will be pleased with. Each person is given £1 or £2 (or more if you can afford it).

Split into groups, depending on the children's ages and meet back, at an agreed time, to exchange gifts. The winner is the one who gives the most happiness.

This game has produced creative fun for our family. Once when we played it, one of our children decided to buy a bottle of lemonade, a packet of cheap biscuits and two cheap supermarket loaves.

When we met up he explained that, as Dad liked nature, we could all sit and feed the birds in the park, and have a drink and biscuit while we watched them. He was the outright winner.

One of the best features of this game is that the children have to think about what someone else would like, which is a welcome break from the egocentric norm.

It requires considerable mental effort and is an excellent exercise in thinking about what each person would like, despite limited funds. Try it and you will be surprised at how much creativity is revealed.

My Experience

I once met a friend and our daughters, then thirteen, wanted to go shopping. My friend had more money and I knew that she would give her daughter money to shop. I couldn't give much to mine so, to avoid embarrassment, I told them about the £1 game and they went off to play it. In the end, we all met up and I was presented with a music tape by Barry Manilow.

The girls said they remembered he was one of my favourites and were so excited when they found it in a charity shop. I looked delighted and grateful, although inwardly my heart sank as I was certainly not a fan of his but I was happy that they were being thoughtful.

Once I had placed it in my bag, they fell about laughing and said that they had got me something else, but they had 20p to spare and wanted to see whether I would pretend to be grateful for the ghastliest gift they could find.

Treasure hunt

This is an excellent game that can be played anywhere and can make a simple activity much more fun. For example, an ordinary snack time can be transformed by making the effort to create a treasure hunt, with the snack being the prize.

Simply make four or five clues of where things could be and then place them around the house or garden, making them suitable for the age and stage of the children. Picture clues work well for young ones.

For a longer activity, you could have two simultaneous treasure hunts, with each group writing the clues for the other group e.g. children and parents. From my experience, this is a painless way to practise reading and writing with your children, and the possibilities are endless.

You could place clues in your local park while the children are in the play area. The treasure hunt is then ready for when they get bored.

If you have a treat, you could tell them that there will be a prize. On the final clue, write that there is something special to be found and they will be much more excited. It only takes about five scraps of paper and a bit of imagination to achieve this.

9

Other ways to sell

Pavement sales

This is an idea we saw in Holland, where children placed everything they wanted to sell on a blanket or tablecloth in their front garden or pavement in front of their house.

They sat next to their goods and people wandered by and bought items for low prices. It was not necessarily for charity but it got rid of things they had grown out of, like a small-scale boot sale.

This is a simple activity which requires minimal preparation but would only work in some areas and needs a parent to supervise. My children loved pavement sales and did them regularly. Sometimes they raised money for charity or themselves; sometimes half and half. It doesn't matter why they are doing it, as long as people know and are not being conned.

The children can make their own advertisements and distribute them around the area the day before or in the morning. You will be inundated with families looking for somewhere to go with their children.

They probably won't want you to be involved, so it is a great excuse to have a cup of tea while you are watching. For some unknown reason, the children will sit on their mats, chat with whoever will talk to them, and play the shop game as they constantly reorganise their ware.

It is a helpful exercise in recycling. Once the idea catches on, your neighbour's children will be doing the same, and you can go along on an outing and buy all the stuff they are chucking out.

However, you must make it a formal event which is clearly advertised and people properly invited, or it can look as if you have sent your children to beg on the street.

My Experience

The only time my children were upset by a pavement sale was when a neighbour asked for all their soft toys and duly paid 10p for each.

The children were thrilled to see that all their much-loved, but outgrown, teddies and soft dolls were going to a good home. So they were somewhat dismayed when he announced, "Thanks so much for these, it is always hard to find something for my dog to chew."

Bring-and-buy sales

We have also organised these more ambitious sales in our house. The title explains it all. People bring things they don't want and buy things they do. The sales are usually for charity as people are less inclined to donate things to make you richer.

It is an excellent activity for children and doesn't require a lot of work. You offer refreshments and your neighbours and friends turn up with stuff they want to get rid of. Your children run around, sorting it all with labelling and pricing. Everyone else sits around, having a good conversation.

It does wonders for the community (a lot of my neighbours met people they didn't know), and everyone gains things they want and gets rid of stuff they don't. At the end of the afternoon, any unwanted goods can be taken to a charity shop. It is an all-round winner.

Just don't be too ambitious and invite so many people that you can't cope with the number of goods they bring.

Uniform shops

School uniforms can be a huge expense when you are on a tight budget. Some schools have their own secondhand shop, which is an invaluable resource. If not, the best solution is to offer to run a uniform sale at the school each term.

The school may agree to store used uniform and parents can be told in advance so that they don't give away the uniform their children grow out of. At each sale, everything can be displayed in the school hall and people can make small donations for items they want.

The advantage of organising the event yourself, is that you can get the first pick of the uniform so that your children are always well-dressed. Schools are usually compliant, as they are parent-led and enable more children to be in uniform.

You can help families struggling with uniforms by allowing them access to the store at other times, and children joining the school can have access to cheap uniforms.

Taste-and-try events

These are relatively simple events to organise.

Make it be a family event and raise money for charity. The children can do it with their friends but will probably need your support.

Decide the theme for a recipe book e.g. main meals under £2. Ask between eight and ten people for their tried and tested recipes, then print a book including them. It will be a fantastic resource for families on a budget and the money can be given to charity.

Plan a convenient time for everyone to arrive at your house, with their cooked recipe. Arrange the food so that it can be tasted before buying a copy of the book.

The book can also be sold to friends who want the recipes or want to donate to charity.

10

Cooking

Cooking is a wonderful productive activity

You have to provide daily meals anyway so, by being creative, you can turn it into an event. Cooking on a budget can be a great activity if you approach it correctly. You don't have to be an excellent cook but you must be savvy.

When I was raising children, we only had recipes in books. It can be great fun to look through these with children, to get ideas and plan meals together.

Now however, there is a proliferation of fantastic recipes online. Search for anything and you will find what you need. You should always add the words 'easy' or 'quick' to the search if you don't want anything too complicated.

There are also lots of YouTube videos that guide you through each step of the recipes. You can use these with your children, especially if you need help to make them yourself. This can be a good experience for children as you are modelling that they can learn any skill they want from the internet.

Ignore the online pictures of perfect-looking cakes and immaculate children. Connect with online communities and meet others on a budget. It is enjoyable to swap great ideas and share thoughts with like-minded individuals.

Another idea is to pair up with another family. You all eat the main course at one house, then go to the other for the dessert. This makes the evening meal into an outing for both families.

Build up your family's recipe book

As you cook with your children, you will build a repertoire of enjoyable recipes that work for you. It is helpful to keep them so that your children can refer to them as they become independent cooks. This can be done online.

I recommend that children get involved in cooking food for the family as young as possible. You do not need special recipe books for children, as they often include recipes no one wants to eat.

Use common sense to keep your children safe. If you use knives, the child can put their hand on top of yours as you cut.

I did not let my children balance on a chair by the work surface, as it felt unsafe. We did a lot of cooking on a plastic tablecloth on the floor. It is much easier to manage a young child and focus on the preparation when you aren't worried that they will fall.

There is no need to worry about making something fantastic. You will find that most children enjoy the creativity and sociability of cooking.

I had a straightforward rice pudding recipe that only used cups and a wooden spoon, so the youngest child made that dessert for the family.

Do not think that children only enjoy making cakes and biscuits, although these are often safe and straightforward. Some children prefer to cook a main course, desserts or make bread. Discover each child's preference, as a lot depends on their character. One may only be interested in the food they can eat immediately. Others may prefer cooking things for a picnic the next day.

Be guided by the children and do not limit them to making the inevitable, but highly delicious, chocolate rice crispy cakes.

Avoid ready-made cake mixes

This is an expensive way of buying ordinary ingredients. Read the side of the packets and you will discover that you are paying a lot for flour and sugar, yet still need to add most of the ingredients.

Enable all children to enjoy cooking by finding ways around any difficulties they have

Some children struggle with various aspects of cooking. I have taught children on the autistic spectrum and adapted the way we did things to make it feel safer for them.

Some hated the feeling of fat being rubbed into flour, so we used knives like scissors and they never had to touch it. Others wanted to cook wearing plastic gloves. If a child hates the messiness of dough, make sure you do that part and then let them handle it when it is a solid mass and ready for kneading. Do whatever works.

Even though you might need to find some solutions, I urge you to let your children cook. Whatever you do, listen to them and ensure that cooking is fun and does not cause distress.

For anyone with non-verbal children, cooking is a fantastic way to communicate. You can share the multi-sensory activity and then eat the food together. If the child hates physical touch, you can mix things in a bowl together with just the spoons touching.

This book is about budgeting but cooking with autistic children and those with sensory issues needs a book of its own.

Cooking can be a whole day's activity

If cooking is something you only do as an extra activity with the children, e.g. making a cake, why don't you let it become a natural part of your day?

It can be fun to cook a whole meal with children and you can involve them in the planning, shopping, table setting, cooking and serving.

Themes

It helps everyone to remain focused if you have a theme for the main meal. The children will come up with plenty of suggestions once they get the idea.

How would you develop an Italian theme, to turn a simple meal into an extraordinary experience?

To make pizza, all you need is flour, oil, cheese, tomatoes, tomato puree, oregano, a tin of tomatoes, onions and dried yeast.

Turn your kitchen into a pizza-making factory, with plenty of chopping, cutting and grating to fill everyone's time.

- Make pizza bases using either a scone or bread base. The latter takes longer and can be a separate activity. When kneading the dough with children, I always put on "We will, we will rock you" by Queen as it helps them to stay focused and establish a good rhythm. Play it twice and they will have kneaded the dough for the right length of time. You can use any music you like with a strong beat.

- Make tomato sauce to cover the pizza.

- Use any toppings e.g. ham, tinned pineapple, salami, etc. Plain cheese and tomato work just as well.

- Make a salad to go with the pizzas; yet more chopping and cutting.

- Make an Italian dressing for the salad.

- Create little Italian flags to label the toppings, using coloured paper or crayons.

- Play Italian music while you are cooking in your "restaurant".

- Make chef's hats for those working in the kitchen area and dress the children as waiters and waitresses for when they serve the food.

- Make placemats with an Italian theme and write name labels for the table.

- Older children can use Google Translate to learn Italian words. Search "English to Italian" and hear the words spoken in Italian. Then swap it by getting them to repeat the word and see if the correct English translation appears.

- Watch a video about Italy on YouTube Kids which should be a safe platform, but I recommend you watch it together.

Can you see that this plan is entirely different from picking up the phone for a pizza delivery? The latter is easier but, if you are on a budget, your children will learn how to cook and have much more fun doing it this way.

Your goal is to end up with children who can cook themselves and, trust me, when they are adults, this will pay off.

Other themes and ideas to consider

- Any country's food e.g. Mexican, American, Greek or Chinese.

- Any colour e.g. rainbow colours or red food only.

- Any shape e.g. all items have to be circular.

- General themes e.g. fireworks, monsters or giants.

Once they know the theme, the children will provide lots of ideas.

Television programmes as inspiration

Copying some of these ideas can also liven up the game.

1. Ready Steady Cook:

Put a set of ingredients in a carrier bag and let the children work out what meal could be made with them.

You might have 6 tomatoes, 6 large potatoes, tomato purée, 1 onion, 1 stock cube, cheese, milk and a packet of minced meat (beef, lamb, turkey, pork, soya or Quorn).

Meal suggestions from these ingredients could be:

- Shepherd's pie with cheese topping

- Moussaka (with tomatoes, not aubergine)

- Jacket potatoes with Bolognese sauce

2. MasterChef:

Older children might enjoy this approach, where they are encouraged to choose a dish and cook it for their family. Complicated recipes are not necessary, just a creative approach to essential ingredients.

Ideas to make mealtime more fun, at no extra cost

- all use chopsticks

- eat blindfolded

- feed each other with only forks

- eat whilst someone reads a story

- eat in time to music

- make up a story together while you eat

- eat with a small spoon

Same food but presented differently

How you present food can make a significant difference to the fun value of the meal.

Use cookie cutters to make attractive sandwiches. Don't forget to use the crusts to make breadcrumbs, as these can be used in lots of recipes e.g. making minced beef go further.

Use cocktail sticks to make vegetable cars, with cucumber slices as wheels attached to small peppers.

Arrange food on a plate to make a caterpillar or any other creature (links can be found on the website). There are many suggestions online that are easy to replicate or adapt.

Make a little go a long way

If you haven't got a lot of fruit or vegetables, you can make it go further by putting them on a cocktail stick and calling it a kebab.

Arrange a dessert in a wine glass to make it look more substantial.

Use smaller plates so it isn't as obvious there isn't much food.

My Experience

Change the setting for the meal

We had a family visit us when I was pregnant, tired and short of money. Although I desperately wanted to see them, I couldn't face the work it entailed. I decided to serve previously frozen fish and chips but thought that it might look like I hadn't made much effort. So I turned the table into a mock fish and chip shop and dished everyone their meal in greaseproof bags and newspaper. It was a fantastic success and the children thought they had arrived in heaven.

The idea's originality hid the fact that I was too tired to do anything else, and the frozen fish, fish fingers and chips did taste better. Best of all, the wrapping got thrown away and there was no washing up.

I recommend this plan to you.

On another occasion, in a railway station, expensive pre-packed meals were on sale. The children were upset that we wouldn't buy them.

The next day, I labelled some cardboard boxes as railway lunches and served the same food as they would typically have on a picnic. We arranged the chairs as if in a railway waiting room and ate our lunch. As a result of the presentation, no one thought it was boring.

School dinners are fun

If you have a larger than usual number of children coming for a meal, one way to cut down on serving everything at the table is to call it the "School Dinners" game.

The food is lined up on a table and the children file past, while you dollop appropriate amounts on their plates. It's a breeze and no one thinks you are being rude as it's just another game.

This works best with, for example, a mash and sausage type meal. For authenticity, my generation would expect a pudding with thin custard.

Hide-and-seek dinners

One summer, I wanted the children to eat out in the garden but we had so many picnics that everyone was fed up with them.

I decided that desperate measures were called for (desperation always precipitates my most creative moments). I made up individual lunches, putting each into a plastic carrier bag and knotting it tightly inside another bag with the child's name on it.

Whilst they played, I hid the bags around the garden. When it was lunchtime, I told them that their food was hidden in the garden. The rule was that no one could eat until everyone had found the bag with their name on it.

This idea worked well. The children enjoyed the hunt, stayed in the garden to eat, and no one realised it was a well-disguised picnic.

Cowboy suppers

Any food tastes better when eaten in an unusual place. When you need budgeting activities, you can make them more exciting for children by introducing variety. Perhaps put up a tent or make one by slinging blankets across a rope.

Serve a cowboy supper which consists of baked beans, potatoes, sausages, or similar. The 'cowboy' bit means outdoors, and young children think it is terrific fun. You can, of course, put a tent up indoors if it is too cold outside.

Picnics and BBQs

These are lifesavers if you are on a budget. It is less evident that you have very little food if you are sitting outdoors and plenty of things are happening around you. As far as possible, get the children to help make the picnic. Make sure that everything packed is easy to eat. You can take a knife and chopping board, but it is only a hassle.

Ideas for a picnic:

- Sandwich faces
- Jacket potatoes wrapped in foil and tea towels to keep them hot
- Hot dog sausages in a food flask then served in bread rolls
- Dips, toppings and pre-cut vegetables
- Soup in a flask
- Lots more ideas online

11

Presents and parties

Stock up all year

When you are short of money, it can be a nightmare working out how to give your child a present they will be pleased with. So, you need to approach this with careful planning.

I had six children with birthdays all close to Christmas. My strategy was to go shopping at every sale during the year and buy something good for each child with a 70% discount. Most people lose interest after Christmas, but I bought lots of things and put them away for the year. Clothes are significantly reduced when they are out of season, so buy them and store them, as it isn't hard to determine what size your child will be by Christmas.

I also stocked up at jumble and boot sales (see Chapter 19: Jumble sales and boot sales). I particularly searched for items in the original wrapper which looked new. When Christmas came, I had lots of presents for each child and could then buy the one thing they really wanted.

The secret is to keep a record of your stash under each child's name.

Present boxes

Even if a present is cheap, it can be turned into something fantastic if you use the right box. The principle is to buy inexpensive things that fill up a lot of space and add one or two props to make it look unique.

These are just suggestions, but once you get the idea, you can make anything according to the interests of your child.

- **Art box**
  If your child is interested in art, you can make them their own art/craft box (see Chapter 4: Art box). Make the container more special by wrapping it up.

- **Cooking box**

  You can make one of these if your child is keen on cooking.

  Print out a few simple recipes and put the ingredients in the box e.g. bread rolls, small cakes, pasta, sauce mix, etc.

  Make a simple apron. In Poundland, buy a few wooden spoons, a plastic mixing bowl and maybe a baking tray.

  Put anything in it that makes it look more special for the child.

  If you want to, you can wrap everything individually inside the box. Once they have opened it, you can help them with the cooking, using their new items.

  You will have saved money if you would have eaten the food anyway, and they feel that they have had a special present.

  Take photos of them opening it and cooking, and they might remember it as their best present ever.

- **Gardening box**

  You can make one of these if your child is keen on gardening.

  Often you can get discarded flowerpots and seed trays which can be washed. Buy some seeds and bulbs and a cheap watering can and tools. A flat growbag will bulk out the present.

When opened, you can grow things together with your child.

- **Post Office box**
  Use a box which can be converted into a post office counter. Fill it with paper, envelopes, a pen, a pencil, a rubber and several of the cheapest stamps. You can buy relatively inexpensive sheets of old stamps on eBay. A cheap receipt book adds to the fun and possibly a stamping set.

  This box can be adapted to be suitable for your child's age.

Buy what you normally do but make it unique

As I raised my children with little money, I never wanted them to feel that they didn't get a lot of presents. So, I used to buy more unique versions of things we used anyway, e.g. a toothbrush in their stockings at Christmas. They needed these anyway, but I paid a bit extra and got special ones, as well as special toothpaste and lovely-smelling soap.

Sometimes on a budget, everything is basic. This system means you can make your child feel special without spending a fortune.

I also discovered that buying a new duvet set is the cheapest way to change a child's room. If you find one with their favourite colours or themes, it looks like a massive present. Pillows can be an excellent complementary present.

My Experience

This idea went spectacularly wrong with my youngest child on her thirteenth birthday. Her favourite colour was pink, and she was obsessed with it.

For her birthday, I bought a pink towel, flannel, bedding, slippers, curtains, and other cheap pink items. The idea was that her room would have a complete makeover on her birthday, and she would be in pink heaven. On the eve of her birthday, I was excited and went to kiss her goodnight.

She explained that now, as she was older, she had gone off pink and wanted turquoise and brown things.

A crushing moment but an amusing memory.

Be happy with less and encourage your child to be satisfied

One option is to explain to your child that they already have so much and maybe they need to be happy with just one present. Possibly set an example and use your birthday to help someone in the community instead of receiving a gift.

We live in a materialistic society and it is hard to break the pressure but it is something we need to consider.

Parties

When you are short of money, it is difficult to throw a party, especially if your child is invited to extravagant parties. You can cut costs by only asking a few children and making the invitations with your child or sending a WhatsApp message. An easy way to acknowledge a gift is to send a WhatsApp photo of your child holding it, with a thank you comment. This is much cheaper than posting cards.

I found my way through this by making my parties different, which reduced the comparisons made by children and parents. I have given a few examples below.

- **Pizza party**
  For this, we provided ready-made pizza bases with different toppings and the children made their own pizzas. This provided an activity and fed everyone relatively cheaply.

  It is easier to have a party in the summer as you can invite children to a birthday picnic and play outdoor games.

- **Pancake party**

  For this, buy some cheap toppings and let your children enjoy making crazy combinations of fillings. You can either make the pancakes in advance and store them between sheets of baking parchment or cook them as you go along. Older children can cook and toss them which provides an activity for them.

- **Film party**

  This can be an inexpensive party. Invite the children to a cinema show and make it clear what the film will be. Have it at a non-meal time e.g. Saturday afternoon.

  Arrange the room with quilts and cushions on the floor so that the children can relax and have fun.

  Give them tubs of popcorn to keep up the theme and serve ice creams in the interval. You can make your own popcorn in a saucepan or microwave cheaply.

- **Construction party**

  Set up your living space with different activities which will work for younger children.

  Fill a large storage crate with out-of-date pasta or foam filling (saved from deliveries) and then put construction toys in it for the children to play with.

Put a pile of play bricks in another area. Download colouring sheets of construction toys. In this example, you could make the food look like cars by adding cucumber wheels. Put construction toys on the table and turn trucks into dishing bowls, using aluminium foil. You may need to borrow some toys from your friends.

This is just one theme but you can choose any theme you like and have play areas for the children to freely move around.

This type of party is easier to manage than one where the children do everything together.

Make ordinary food look special

This is another trick at parties e.g. turn the rolls into a group of sailboats by cutting them in half and inserting them with a cocktail stick and a triangle of coloured paper. Another suggestion is to put fish fingers in long rolls, with the top sticking out, and call them "shark fins".

If you aren't a good baker and can't afford the shop-bought cakes, make sure you make a themed cake so that the child is more excited about the theme than your lack of skill. The other trick I used was to put a lot of tinsel around the base of the cake which made a small cake look more significant and expensive when you light the candles. Be careful you don't set fire to the tinsel.

Decorations

These can be expensive, but balloons are the cheapest way to make a room look special. You can also use them in party games and, if you string them individually, give one to each child as they leave.

You can make bunting or paper chains from sheets of wrapping paper, which can be an effective activity with your child before the party.

There are lots of templates online from which you can personalise colouring sheets and placemats for each child. You could use coloured paper for this or, if you use white paper, the children could colour theirs as a party activity.

You know how tight the budget is and how hard you work to make your child feel special, so avoid comparing yourself with anyone else. Put your energy into making the party enjoyable as all the children will remember is whether they had fun.

When the children leave

At some parties, children are given expensive party bags and gifts. You can be super creative and, as well as giving each child a balloon and piece of cake to take home, you could make it more special with the following ideas:

- create an adoption certificate for each guest and attach it to a cheap or free soft toy

- create a reporter's pack for each guest by buying a cheap multipack of notebooks and pens

- make homemade playdough and put it in a take-away tub for each guest

When your child is invited to parties

This can be difficult if you are short of money. I recommend that you have a stock of presents which you buy in the sales. When your child is invited to a party, they can choose which present they think their friend would like. They can make a card as these can also be expensive.

Change the rules at Christmas

Don't fall into the trap of getting into debt because of the media pressure to spend lots of money. Work out your budget and stick to it. You can make Christmas fun by starting a new tradition and doing anything you like. Have a pyjama day if it is easier.

I know a family who said they would each have some-thing new, something second-hand and something handmade. This idea was a challenge but it worked for their budget.

Another idea to reduce financial pressure is to agree on four presents for each person: something you want, something you need, something to wear and something to read.

Christmas food

With a small budget, the tradition of eating expensive food at Christmas is difficult but there are ways to make it memorable without spending a lot, e.g. you can choose a day when you all eat your favourite foods.

If you are hosting others, ask them to bring part of the meal as it is unrealistic for you to produce everything.

Why not spread out the cost by buying something each week leading up to Christmas?

Investigate your local supermarkets' saving stamp schemes. Some have good bonuses and can make Christmas more affordable.

Christmas presents

It may be the time to agree with your wider family not to exchange presents. A bit of honesty could take the pressure off everyone.

Another idea is to set a price limit and see how creative you can be.

Suggestions of games to make presents more fun but cheap:

- Charity shop or Poundshop presents only – a friend of mine buys the ghastliest thing she can find for less than £3, as she and her brother have a year-long quest to find a gift to outdo each other in the ghastliness

- Secret Santa – a price limit is agreed and each person buys a present for another person in the group

Poundshop challenge

I have always been a fan of the poundshops but you have to look carefully to get bargains. My secret is to shop there in July because there will be different stock by Christmas and no one will know how much you spent.

I play what I call "The National Trust Game". If you can imagine an object on sale in a National Trust gift shop, it will meet the criteria. When gift-wrapped, with tissue, it will become a beautiful present. This works particularly well for notebooks and candles.

Another trick is to combine two or three cheap items to look like an attractive coordinated present e.g. £1 face mask, £1 bubble bath and £1 candle together can make an expensive-looking pamper pack.

12

Water play

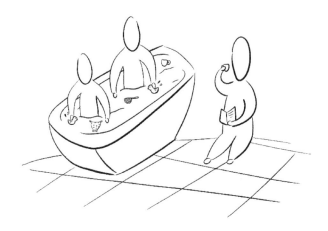

The best thing about water is that it is almost free. The amount you use is negligible for the tremendous number of play activities it offers.

A great advantage of water play is that you can relax, knowing that your child is learning about science. There is a place for water play for all ages, although you need to make it appropriate for each child.

Confession

The following activity works like magic. I discovered it when I was desperate to read a magazine.

There were times with young children (at one stage, I had four children under the age of six) when all I wanted was to have twenty minutes to have a cup of tea and read a magazine. You should never have a hot drink close to children but, it seemed that as soon as I had a cup in my hand, the children came to me as though it had magnetic qualities.

I will share my plan with you.

Put the kettle on. Collect any non-breakable containers from the kitchen cupboard that can be used to pour, sieve and scoop. Run the bath and add a few drops of gentle shampoo or bubble bath with a few drops of food colouring (this is optional). Make the tea and have the magazine ready. Put the children into the bath.

You now have twenty minutes of bliss. You can safely drink your tea and read your magazine on the floor next to the bath, as your children learn about science.

The novelty factor keeps them exploring as you have introduced objects they don't usually play with. Coloured water adds to the fun and distinguishes this from their standard bath time when the goal is to wash them. The aim here is for you to have twenty minutes to yourself and feel human again.

The only rule is that the water must stay in the bath. This is much more fun for the children than when you are hovering over them trying to wash their hair.

You can read what you like but, as this is confession time, I must admit that when I was very stressed, nothing worked as well for me to zone out as "Take a Break".

I have never been enthusiastic about young children playing with water while standing at a sink. It seems dangerous for them to balance on a chair or stool. It is safer in a bath and you can all relax better.

You can make it even more enjoyable by putting on music while they play. You can play with them when you don't need a break but let the activity be child-led.

Activities with water

There are unlimited activities you can do with water, so here are a few ideas to get you thinking.

- **Balloon water bombs**

  This is best played outdoors. It is possible to buy small water balloons but it's not necessary, as you can fill any size of balloon with water and use it as a ball. It has interesting properties and is hard to catch without bursting it.

  Once you have made a set of water bombs, you can play any of the following games:

  - throw them at each other but have a change of clothes ready

  - hang them, then try to break them by hitting them, a cheap version of piñata

  - set challenges, for example:

  Who can balance a water bomb on their head the longest?

  How high can a few of you bounce a water bomb in the air using a large picnic cloth as a launch pad?

  Who can throw a water bomb the furthest without it exploding?

  Who can make their water bomb explode first?

  Try playing 'water bomb' football, netball or volleyball.

Don't forget to clean up broken balloon pieces after play to avoid litter and harm to animals or the environment.

- **Empty spray bottles**
  Rinse these thoroughly and fill them with water, and they can be used as a wonderful garden game, chasing each other to spray them.

- **Floating and sinking**
  Collect as many small objects as possible and then guess whether they will float or sink. Use a washing-up bowl of water on a mat on the floor so that everyone can see.

- **Paper boats**

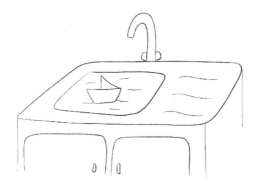

A great challenge is to make a boat that stays afloat using a sheet of paper. You can experiment yourself or search "Make a simple paper boat" for ideas online. This game can be played in the bath, sink or a bowl on a table.

You can also turn bottle lids into boats.

Enjoy making the boats sink by pouring water into them or use spray bottles and see how many squirts will sink them.

- **Washing the toys**
  Encourage children to wash their toys, as it is surprising how filthy they can get. A bowl of water with washing-up liquid provides a few happy minutes and achieves a lot.

- **Bubble wars**
  An inexpensive activity that can make a bit of a mess but is a lot of fun is putting a bowl on a towel between you and a child. Add a small amount of water and washing-up liquid to the bowl. You both have a straw and the goal is to blow bubbles. Keep going until bubbles are over the top of the bowl, and then blow them onto the other person's side for bonus points.

- **Washing-up bowls of water**
  Fill a bowl with water and cover the children with plastic aprons. Give them any type of container and let them get on with it. Most children don't need to be told what to do, as they automatically play. You can model play if they are struggling and lead them verbally.

Warm water will allow them to play for longer. If the weather is warm enough, you can put them in swimming clothes.

A squirt of washing-up liquid or bubble bath can be added to liven it up.

A few drops of food colouring can be added, although beware that it may stain.

- **Limbo**

  If you aren't on a water meter, use a hose to spray water for children to limbo underneath. If you are on a meter, let them go under the hose and give them a quick spray at the end.

  Tip:

  Play this at the end of the day in clothes that need to be washed anyway. Use towels that also need a wash, otherwise, this game generates too much needless washing.

- **Activities with ice**

  Freezing water adds a new dimension to play. It is helpful to have lots of ice cubes and, for some of the projects, you will need a bagful. You can get cheap ice cube trays with different shapes that are fun to use, but it is an unnecessary expense to buy ready-made ice cubes from supermarkets.

  If you have old ice trays, you can add colouring before you freeze them. Then let children make sculptures or play on a tray, watching the ice cubes melt as they push them around.

You can also find tiny things and freeze them, like toy farm animals or beads, and then let the children move them around till they melt and the object is freed.

Another idea is to put objects into a balloon, then fill it with water and freeze it. This will produce ice balls and it is great fun to find ways to break them down to recover the objects.

- **Ice art**
  Put powder paint onto a thin card (recycled packaging) before placing ice cubes on it. It is fun to melt the ice cube while you push it around on the paint. This could be done outdoors or on well-covered tables, as it is messy. Acrylic paint can be used but the powder mixes with the melted ice water and it is more fun.

When finished, leave the card to dry and you will have a creative ice picture.

Tip:
Do not let the children handle ice when it comes out of a freezer, as they can get ice burns, but leave it to melt for a few minutes. You can use tongs or cocktail sticks to move the ice around if you don't want the children to touch it, although this detracts from the sensory nature of this activity.

13

Making a mess on purpose

Embrace the mess

Something ordinary can be made special if you change the usual rules. If you are one of those people who insists that children don't make a mess, try giving them times when they can. Some excellent mixtures can be made for minimal cost and produce hours of play, but they do create a mess.

One tip is to use towels or bedding, which need washing, as a cloth for the activities and then wash them afterwards.

Ensure the children are covered if you want their clothes to stay clean. I found that old shirts were far more effective than conventional aprons. Simply cut or turn the sleeves to the correct length and put the shirts on the children back to front.

Make sure you cover anything precious, use trays to contain the activity and make clearing-up part of the fun.

Wherever possible, let the children help you make the mixture, as this will extend the activity and make it more enjoyable for them.

There are many recipes online and demonstrations on YouTube, but I will include a few basic ones in this chapter for quick reference.

Food colouring and other effects

In the recipes, food colouring is optional. It is much easier to use a colouring paste than a liquid. Unfortunately, some colouring can stain clothes, especially red, so I prefer to leave the mixture plain.

If you add colour, ensure that the children work on a tray or use shiny paper to prevent staining. If you make the dough red, yellow and blue, the children will learn about primary colours and be able to form new ones.

Blackcurrant-flavoured tea bags dissolve in water to make a non-staining colour, although you need about three bags.

You could add glitter for a different effect.

Add a scent, such as rose or lavender, to make your mixture more interesting.

Messy mixture recipes

• Cornflour paste

This is a simple activity but is stupendously messy.

Ingredients:
1 cup cornflour
¾ cup water

Method:
Add the water gradually to the cornflour and keep stirring until it is mixed and makes a smooth paste with a thick consistency. This takes trial and error and will be correct when you can roll a small amount (about the size of a 50p coin) into a ball.

Place the mixture onto a plastic tray, large plate, or glass bowl, and then let the children push and poke it, as they play.

Rough handling of the mixture produces a solid mass but becomes a liquid when you stop poking it and the goo pours through your fingers. The possibilities of playing with this are endless and it can produce a wonderful playing time and mess, eventually becoming a powder that can be vacuumed.

You can store it when it is dry and ready to use again just by adding water. The mixture produces a squidgy sensation that I have never felt with another potion. It is therapeutic and relaxing.

- **Playdough**
  This works just as well as anything you can buy.

  Ingredients:
  4 cups flour
  1 cup salt
  1½ tbsp oil
  1½ cups water
  food colouring (optional)

  Method:
  Mix the flour and salt, then gradually add the water and oil. Mix the dough with your hands until smooth and knead it well into a ball. Food colouring may be added.

  Seal the playdough in a plastic bag and place it in the fridge for about an hour.

• One minute playdough

This stores well in a plastic bag and can be reused.

Ingredients:

½ cup salt
1 cup flour
1 tbsp cream of tartar
1 tbsp oil
I cup boiling water
food colouring (optional)

Method:

Put the dry ingredients in a bowl and mix well with the hot water. This should be done by an adult, as it is hot.

When cooled, the children can play with it.

• Salt Dough

This is a great crafting medium for models e.g. Christmas decorations. It is fun to handle, easy to make and can be stored longer than most mixtures.

Ingredients:

4 cups flour
1 cup salt
1 – 1½ cups water
food colouring (optional)

Method:

Put the flour and salt in a bowl. Add 1 cup of water and either use your hands or a spoon to mix. If dry, add more water until your mixture is moist and sticking together.

Let the children shape the dough. Once a model is made, leave it to dry and harden. To make it last longer, bake it at 100^0C until pale brown.

If they don't want to keep the shapes, mix them and put them into an airtight container in the fridge as they can be used again.

• **Bubble mix**

Beware when you mix this, as it is very bubbly. I recommend that you make it the day before it is used.

Ingredients:

½ cup washing-up liquid

5 cups water

1 cup salt

2 tbsp glycerine

Method:

Add the washing-up liquid to the water. If you have hard water, it may work better with bottled water.

Add 2 tablespoons glycerine.

Blow this bubble mixture through any hooped shapes you can find. They can be made using pipe cleaners.

Playing with mud

Mud is easy to make and fun to play with outside.

Put soil into a bucket or old washing-up bowl and mix it with water. Make sure the children feel it to get the consistency they want. It can be great fun to spread liquid mud around, yet more solid mud can be used to build shapes.

Older children may want to focus on making small mud bricks. In hot weather, you can leave them to dry and use them to make huts.

Set your family a challenge e.g. make a miniature mud village.

If it is warm enough and you want to avoid washing lots of clothes, this is an excellent activity in swimwear.

Messy feet

Pour child-friendly paint onto a tray. Each child can then use this to print their footprint or handprint onto a piece of paper. Why don't you make a family picture of all your hands, in varying colours?

Unless you are courageous, this activity is best done outdoors.

Papier-mâché

This is easy to make and can be used for various art projects. It can be made straightforward for young children, or a more complex activity for older children.

You will need a balloon, paintbrush, newspaper or any non-glossy paper and homemade glue, paste or PVA glue.

Be aware that shop-bought wallpaper paste contains fungicide and newspaper print can also be toxic. These are not suitable for young children as they often put their fingers in their mouths.

Homemade glue (thin version)
Mix ¼ cup of flour with cold water until it is smooth. Boil 5 cups of water in a saucepan and then pour this onto the flour mix in a bowl. Bring this back to a boil and stir for 2-3 minutes until it thickens. Cool before using.

Homemade paste (thicker version)
Use 1 cup of flour to 3 cups of water.

PVA glue
If you use PVA glue, you will need to water it down.

Before you start, cover every surface you are working on as the glue goes everywhere and the newspaper print can stain. Make sure the children are wearing suitable aprons or art shirts (see the beginning of this chapter).

You can make a papier-mâché version of virtually any shape. If you want to cover a plate or a bowl, make sure to coat it with a little Vaseline, oil or washing-up liquid before you cover it with mâché and glue. Otherwise, you won't be able to remove the object from the mâché. Cling film can be used but it can result in a mottled appearance.

Method

Tear the paper into strips about 15cm by 3cm, or smaller pieces for finer projects. Using the paintbrush, apply glue to both sides of each strip. Put the strips onto the inflated balloon (or another object) and keep smoothing down as you go along.

Continue until you have covered the shape with a thin layer of paper. It is best to do about two or three layers at a time and allow them to dry overnight before adding another few layers.

Continue until the papier-mâché is the desired thickness.

If you want to add different shapes, you can use masking tape to secure pieces of cardboard and then layer over the top with papier-mâché.

Once it is dry, the balloon will come away when it is burst but make sure you do not burst it before the covering is completely dry, or it will collapse.

You now have a solid balloon shape. You could perhaps cut this in half lengthways to make masks.

Pulped papier-mâché

This method produces a clay-like mixture which can be used for sculptural work.

To make the pulp, tear up the newspaper into small pieces and soak them in water overnight. Drain the mixture and then boil it for about 25 minutes or until the fibres start to break up. Sieve the mixture and stir with a wooden spoon so that all the threads in the paper break up. Mix glue into the pulp until it is like clay. Apply this mixture to objects or mould it into freestyle shapes.

Once dry, it can be painted.

Keeping the things your children make

The reality is that no one will have space to keep everything their children make. Hence, the secret is to save a precious few but keep the rest for a while, before moving them out of sight. You could photograph them before you bin them.

Never bin them where the children might find them or they will want them back.

You could keep a record of their art online, perhaps as a slideshow. When my children were small, we didn't have the luxury of mobile phones and all our photographs had to be printed. I stored as much art as I could but, when it came out of the loft thirty years later, it bore little resemblance to the original. My children couldn't understand why I had kept it.

14

Language

Using words

Whatever else is increasing in price, words are still free and it is important to maximise language activities with your children to get them through life.

WRITING

Send notes to your children

It is lovely to send notes with positive words to your children.

- hide messages under their pillows, stick them on their doors, and put them in their lunchboxes

- write a letter to your child to tell them how special they are – these gifts are priceless

- encourage your child to write notes or draw pictures for people

Write a story about your child

It rarely works that you can ask a child to write a story and they get on with it (although apparently, some children do). However, as we have already said, children are self-centred by nature and I have found that their motivation is increased if you ask them to write a story about themselves.

Buy a notepad or create a book using A4 paper and a stapler. Make it size-appropriate for the age and stage of your child. Sit with them and tell them that you are going to make up a story about them. This can be great fun when it involves learning adventurous vocabulary.

Discuss what they would like their book to be about. It can, of course, be entirely imaginary.

Content suggestions

- My day
- I like

- I don't like
- The day it snowed
- My family
- The day I was king/queen
- A scary thing happened

How to present it

Once written, you can illustrate it together. Keep it simple and don't worry about the presentation. It is destined to be one of their favourite stories because it is about them. No one else needs to see it so don't be put off if it isn't a particularly exciting or interesting story.

Some children love this activity and may want to write a series. Put the date on the back and, when they stop reading it, put it somewhere safe as it will be a fantastic memory when they are older.

Another option is to make up your own story about your child. This can be special and you can have a great deal of fun. You could write it and let your child add the illustrations.

Make stories as computer presentations

The child's story can be presented on a computer, with clip art and photos added. I have used PowerPoint for presentations but there are others. Office suites can be downloaded free of charge.

If you don't have the technology, don't be put off. The plain paper and pencil method works just as well.

Photographic records

Always take digital photographs when you go out with your children, as you can later make a record of your trip. The quality of phone photos and videos is fantastic and they can be incorporated into a production.

Most children have excellent computer skills, so encourage them to make a presentation about their trip or activities to show the whole family. You might like to print some off and make an old-fashioned photo album.

Personalised scrapbooks

A scrapbook is a highly decorated record of an event or theme, usually including photographs, memorabilia and some writing. They can be sophisticated productions but a simple approach is sufficient for our purposes.

If you take your child somewhere, you can later make a story scrapbook of the day. Plan ahead and keep train tickets, brochures and leaflets which can be included.

You can buy a relatively inexpensive scrapbook or you can make your own, using sugar paper or brightly coloured paper and staples. Making them adds to the fun. Scrapbooks are traditionally quite large but they can be any size you want to make.

Writing and images make a scrapbook personal. Include photographs, leaflets and any other memorabilia you can collect. There are plenty of online scrapbooking ideas and free resources you can download to add.

I suggest that you use coloured photocopies of photographs in a scrapbook. They will not look as good but you cannot expect children to keep the originals unmarked, with all the glue and colouring involved in a scrapbook. Put the photographs in an album.

Remember that an outing is primarily for fun. Although the child may learn from it, do not spoil everything by forcing it into an educational experience. Teachers, and those working with children, tend to spoil the enjoyment by making the children write about it afterwards or by encouraging them to read everything out loud as they go along.

If you are making a scrapbook, do all the writing and let the child do the sticking and cutting, if they prefer.

Be guided by the child's genuine interests and enthusiasm.

Personalised scrap box

You could make this instead of a scrapbook, using a container like a shoe box. Decorate the outside and then fill it with relevant objects and notes about the event. This requires less glue and might be preferred by a child who doesn't like books.

READING

Read out loud to your children

Reading a night-time story has long been a recommended method of settling children at bedtime and is an excellent activity if your child enjoys it. Stories and poems can be read at any time and provide a perfect and free activity.

When I served a dessert to my family, I saved mine for later and read poems or a story which made mealtimes special. We ended up with some particular favourites. I am not suggesting that you do this at every mealtime but it is great fun when done occasionally.

Some children enjoy books being read aloud. Whenever we went on holiday, we took a holiday book and I read a chapter after every evening meal.

You can use your computer or phone to record yourself reading, then make an audiobook for your child.

Join a library or form your own

If you haven't already discovered the local library, now is the time to get your children enrolled. It is the most valuable source of an extensive range of books and magazines, and it is free to join.

A trip to the library is an exciting outing. It is not meant to be a time when you only swap books. Take time to sit with your children and read with them.

The overall aim is that your children will love books and the choice in a library is phenomenal. You may offer gentle guidance but do not prescribe which books a child should read.

Find out what is being offered at your library as there are often story times, activities and reading programmes during school holidays. I have yet to find a library that doesn't produce a massive range of free and excellent resources.

Some children don't enjoy reading but they could listen to stories using online audio resources. Children need to develop an understanding of language as well as speak it. So choose audiobooks that are slightly more challenging than the level your child can read.

However, consider your child's choice and don't just choose books you like.

I spent many fruitless hours looking for lost library books until we decided to keep them in a separate container to be returned to, rather than letting the children put all the books in their bedroom. Make a list of the books you take out so that you do not receive embarrassing email reminders.

It is also possible to find smaller 'libraries' on Facebook or neighbourhood groups, including phone box hubs and book swap facilities.

If nothing exists where you live, you could set one up. It is possible to buy cheap books on eBay and in charity shops.

TALKING

Talk to your children

It is good to do this as much as possible.

- have fun sessions where you tell jokes or play games with tongue twisters

- use pretend phones with young children

- each person changes the tone of their voice and whispers or speaks without moving their lips

- talk about what you are doing with your child

- talk to them about their activities, listen to them and enjoy the conversation
- aim to add an unusual new word each day to your vocabulary

It seems strange that we spend the early years encouraging our children's speech, and then spend the next few years wishing they would be quiet. Talk is free and yet it can help you to forge deep bonds with your family.

Go out to talk

Parenting can be a lonely business at times. Take your children to places where they, and you, can talk. Children's centres and toddler groups are cheap or free to attend. Some people find it hard to chat with others but I guarantee that, when you start a conversation, you will find other people who are desperate to talk. This is all free and will greatly enrich you and your child.

15

Angels and acts
of random kindness

Being kind is free

This is a wonderfully free activity, as well as being intrinsically important.

As parents, it is important to remember that we want our children to be kind so it will help to find free activities that encourage this. While children are engaged in thinking about others, it is less evident that you don't have much money. Parents need to set an example, so any activity that encourages children to think about others usually means that you are also involved.

Some children seem kinder by nature and are easy to encourage. Others seem more self-centred and it will be more challenging to get them to participate. However, it is worth persevering as they are the ones we need to encourage most.

Do activities to encourage kindness

We used to play a game called "Angels" but you can name it anything. The idea is that you become a lovely person for someone else.

We put our names on a piece of paper and drew out a name, which was supposed to be secret. We then had to do kind things for that person but not let on that we were their angel.

In reality, we all knew exactly what was going on. Still, it encouraged the children to be creative and not to boast about their actions. We joined in as parents and sent caring cards or left a little gift under their pillows. We talked with the children about what they could do and what would make the other person feel special. They were very creative and it drew out their better natures.

You can decide how long the game goes on – an hour, half a day or a day. Theoretically, you could string it out over days, but I have to say none of mine ever lasted longer than a day.

It can be great fun and, although it can only be played with willing participants, it does change the dynamics of a relationship, albeit for a short time. It is a good feeling if one of your children is thinking about how they can improve your day. It is a more straightforward game to play with a larger family but you could join another family for the day to play it.

Since we raised our children, there has been a rise in the popularity of the "Naughty Elf" at Christmas. He is supposed to get up to all kinds of mischief in the house for the whole of December. There seems to be a divide among parents, with some thinking it is an awful thing to do as it encourages bad behaviour. I fortunately never had this dilemma but, as a grandparent, I have an awesome elf who goes around doing kind things in the house.

If any of your children are passionate about a charitable cause, encourage them to do a fundraising activity. It is helpful to think about people less fortunate as it is a better focus than reflecting on your own small budget. It is good for your children to learn that they can make a difference to others, and any activity to raise money means that they are purposefully occupied. They learn a lot about themselves and it develops their entrepreneurial skills.

Random acts of kindness

There has been a considerable rise in what is popularly known as Random Acts of Kindness (RAOK) or Acts of Random Kindness (ARK). A search on the internet will give you plenty of groups encouraging these activities.

The idea is that you find ways to make others happy and not necessarily be thanked for your service. The person receiving kindness should be encouraged to pass it on.

It can be fun to introduce this idea to your family and, as a group, encourage each other to find ways to make people happier. Your children may already be familiar with it, as the idea is being used in many schools.

There are endless suggestions online and social media groups encourage each other by posting photographs of their actions to make people smile or feel good.

Ideas for random acts of kindness

I will give you twenty which you can use to start a discussion but your children will probably come up with better ones that work in your situation.

1. Tidy someone else's mess without saying anything.

2. Make a card for someone and tell them why they are special or what you like about them.

3. Cook biscuits or cakes and take them to a neighbour.

4. Talk to an older person when you are shopping.

5. Smile at everyone you pass and then count how many smiles are returned. Add "Have a great day" and see what happens.

6. Take gloves when you go out, then pick up rubbish and put it in a bin.

7. Clean someone's shoes without being asked.

8. Sweep the path outside someone's house.

9. Ask if you can help someone unload their shopping trolley onto the conveyor belt.

10. Make a drink for everyone in the family.

11. Clean something in the house.

12. Read a story to someone.

13. Write a letter or send an email to someone. Use a poem or quote from the internet If you don't know what to write.

14. Older children can write positive comments on social media posts.

15. Send a text to someone you don't usually connect with to check how they are.

16. If you can knit or sew, make a small object and leave it in a public place with a note to explain that you made it to make the receiver happy.

17. Create bookmarks with a colourful design and give them to someone.

18. Help wildlife by making a 'bug hotel' out of items you find on the ground in a park or woods.

19. Let someone go in front of you when in a queue.

20. Take something to a charity shop to be reused.

16

Sleepovers

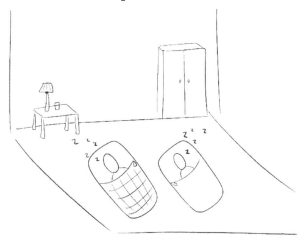

I was enthusiastic about sleepovers and found them to be positive experiences. They are tremendous, and almost free, experiences which give your child opportunities to celebrate with their friends.

However, there are some pitfalls to avoid. Some parents would not entertain the idea of having another child for the night or of letting their child sleep anywhere else. Indeed, in recent years there has been an increased awareness of safeguarding which might affect your decision. If this is you, then skip this chapter.

I have always regarded it as a free source of entertainment for my children and a way of deepening friendships. They can sleepover at any age, but I found that it was a more successful activity when my children were over six years old. My golden rule was that, if I didn't get a good night's sleep, then that child would not be invited over again for a long time.

Pick your child and their parent carefully, as you need to know them both very well. You also need to know who else will be staying in the house with your child.

It doesn't have to be overnight

You can compromise by inviting children for the evening, with their pyjamas and sleeping bags, but ask the parents to collect them later, so that they sleep at home. They can return the following morning for breakfast. This arrangement works well for anxious children, and you will get more sleep.

Make sure you get some sleep

The word sleepover contains ambiguity. With the wrong child, it can mean that sleep is over, and no one will get any because the child is fretting with homesickness or ransacking your house.

Tips for successful sleepovers

- Before you accept a child, make sure you have their parent's telephone number with their agreement to be available and, if their child is upset, they will collect them. You do not want to be left with a troubled child.

- Check if there are any medical issues you should be aware of, including allergies.

- Ask the children to bring sleeping bags or quilts. You can say that it is so that they feel more secure, which is a helpful spin-off, but the reality is that you do not want extra washing.

- Sometimes a small group of children works well if they are good friends.

- Consider the best room for them, which may not be a bedroom as your sleep may be disturbed. They are unlikely to sleep all night, as they will be excited.

- Stay calm and remember that this is the stuff memories are made of.

- Let the children try out their ideas even if it doesn't look like a good plan to you. They will put up with anything if it was their suggestion.

- This is when you can let the children watch films endlessly, but make sure that the correct age category is being viewed as you are responsible for other people's children.

- Put away anything precious but don't make it obvious so that the children don't think you expect them to play roughly.

My Experience

For sleepovers, one of my children always converted our lounge into a camp, using towels and sheets. His friends would duly arrive with their sleeping bags and happily sleep on the floor.

If we had announced that they were not allowed to sleep in their comfortable beds for the night but had to lie under a sheet behind the settee with their noses squashed against a wall, Childline would probably have received a call.

- Put out snacks and food you are happy for them to eat. Make it clear that they are not allowed to eat anything else, as you do not want your cupboards to be ransacked and next week's dinners eaten.

- You may prefer to give them a late-night snack before you go to bed and leave some biscuits out.

- Before going to bed, make sure they are comfortable, knowing that half the fun is that they will play and chat the minute you have gone. Just pretend you don't know that and go to bed relaxed, knowing they are enjoying themselves and it isn't costing you anything.

- I expect them to stay in the room they are sleeping in, but leave the lights on so that they can find you if they need anything.

- Generally, let your child organise things as they will know what the other children like. You can offer to read or settle them if any are homesick.

- Do not give too much responsibility to your child at the beginning of the sleepovers, but gradually increase it as they have more. If things go wrong, make sure you both learn from it.

I always made my children clear up afterwards. They soon got the hang of it and quickly discovered the best friends to invite.

A sleepover can be a cheaper alternative to celebrate a birthday if you can't afford a party. You can make it special by hanging balloons and serving popcorn during the film.

In the morning, I made a special breakfast and told them that the breakfast bar would be open once everything was sorted. That sounds so much more friendly than, "There will only be food once you have tidied up."

Some people allow children to stay in tents in the garden overnight. Personally, I don't think that they are close enough for safety, so we got around this by saying that they could have supper and camp until late before coming inside for the night. I agreed that if they woke up and it was light, they could return to the tent.

A lot depends on your situation but that always worked for us. The underlying principle here is to relax the usual bedtime routine and let your children have some fun during the night.

If your children are young, put a clock in a prominent position and keep putting it forward without them realising it. Without other information, they will think that you allowed them to stay up until one in the morning.

The morning after the sleepover can be just as important as the night itself. Children are often tired and will need food and drink to recharge their batteries. If it isn't a special celebration, make sure you have simple breakfast foods like cereal, toast and juice available.

If you have agreed for someone to collect the children, give them a precise time so that you can plan your day accordingly.

In conclusion, a sleepover can be a fun and memorable experience for children. As free entertainment, it can be an excellent opportunity to strengthen existing friendships and create new ones. However, it's essential to be careful when choosing which children to invite and make sure that you and your child feel comfortable with the arrangement.

By setting clear expectations and rules, you can ensure that the sleepover is a success and that everyone has a good time.

Extra safety idea

If you allow your child to sleep over at another child's house, it might be helpful to have a code word that only you and your child know. This can be used when they phone to say goodnight and, for whatever reason, they want you to come and get them.

A code word can be useful in other situations e.g. if anyone told the children we had sent them or asked them to do something, they would know that it was genuine if the person could tell them the code word. The children knew to refuse any request if the word was not given.

17

Catalogues

Stock up on catalogues and magazines

These are some of the best free resources for images and are often placed at the entrance of shops you can't afford. I would advise you to pick up two copies, so that you can make more activities with matching pictures. Also, by cutting out an image, you lose the one on the back of it.

Make sure you don't read them and wish you had more money, as that is counterproductive. Instead, use them in free activities to develop your child's language and imagination.

You can pick up some for free at shops like Argos and IKEA. However, it is more ecologically friendly to utilise magazines and catalogues which would have been discarded so, if your friends have any to pass on, you can use them. When you ask others, you will discover that most people are happy to pass them on.

Children often enjoy looking through catalogues and talking about what they would like out of them.

Endless activities which include pictures

I devised various activities to get more out of the magazines and catalogues I collected.

- For younger children, you can make your own card games. If you have two identical catalogues, you can make matching pictures and snap games. Cut paper into suitably shaped cards and then stick on your pictures.

- Playing cards make a handy set of readymade bases. You can stick them together face-to-face and use them for your new activity. Ask for packs of cards people are throwing out or get them at a jumble sale.

- Playing cards are a very cheap activity with a high play value and can liven up lots of other games.

- Hide the cards around the room and then ask the child to find them and lay them in a correct sequence.

- Play matching games for younger children, using fewer cards. Older children can arrange the whole set, timed against the clock. Or you can put on a piece of music and see if they can set the cards out in order before the music ends.

- Play simple card games with your children. Google "card games for kids" and check the rules on the internet if you don't know them.

- In an ideal world, you can get the children to help you make the cards. But if that doesn't work, it is a therapeutic activity once they are in bed.

- You can play a matching category game where cards are similar but not identical e.g. images of two different beds. This can be done with groups of images, so you could make sets of cards of "kitchen items" or "clothes".

- Lay out groups of cards and include one that doesn't belong to the set, then let the child guess the "Odd one out".

- Create a game where the first person who gets the whole group of cards is the winner; a catalogue version of "Happy Families."

- With paired cards, you can play the "Pairs" memory game where you put them face-down and try to remember where the matching images are.

- For a language game, find something in the catalogue for each letter of the alphabet. Put the picture on the front and the letter on the back. Ask your child to use them to spell their name, etc.

- If you have small enough images, you can make number cards with the correct number of objects on the card.

Challenges for older children

They are less likely to be excited about the homemade card games, but you can still set the following challenges from the catalogues.

- Imagine you have to furnish a bedroom for a boy/girl of (choose an age). Cut out and stick onto paper the items you would put in the room.

- Set a budget for this to add to the fun for more able children.

Not all children will do this activity, but some play it endlessly and ask you to make up another child for them to play it again. It can last ages, generating conversation and developing their imagination. It is also fun to pretend to spend money.

Avoid asking the child to design their own bedroom as this may make them dissatisfied with what they have.

You can make the challenge more interesting by asking them to design a room for a child who hates blue or who must have spotty patterns.

You can be as creative as you like and it can be relaxing to do this activity simultaneously with your child so that you can talk about what you are doing rather than just watching them.

My Experience

I once played this with my children and they had a wonderful time filling a child's bedroom with every conceivable gadget and toy in the catalogue.

It wasn't until near the end that they realised the child didn't have a bed.

Similarly, with an Argos catalogue, you can suggest that they choose ten toys for a child who has just arrived in this country and has none. Don't ask them to choose the things they would most like, as it won't help your situation.

With a clothes catalogue, you can make holiday pages. The child chooses a person and then cuts out all the clothes they could take with them on holiday. They can also select the suitcase, etc. This could be done as a family activity, with each person packing a different suitcase. You can mount the pictures on paper or put them into an envelopes labelled "suitcase".

Also with a clothes catalogue, you can cut out pictures of items which go in a clothes shop and play all sorts of shopping games. You could cut out pictures of models and have a fashion show.

Magazine images can be inspirational. Your child may simply want to cut out and arrange pictures they like. Alternatively, they may be more creative if you give them a theme e.g. to make a red collage which can include sections of text cut out to add comments to the images.

18

Keeping the house clean

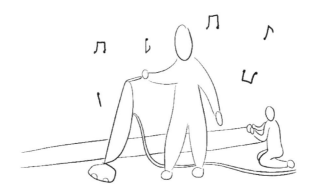

Cleaning is unavoidable

No matter how motivated you are to have quality time with your children, there may be occasions when you also need to clean your house. It would be fantastic if you could afford a cleaner, but you probably can't. You can turn the experience into a free activity. It is important that children are involved and, with effort, it does not have to be boring.

Make your own cleaning materials

Greater ecological expectations mean that there are plenty of recipes for making your own polish, room freshener, surface cleaners, and even oven cleaner. The basic requirements are bicarbonate of soda, a few essential oils (lemon and tea tree seem to be the most favoured), white vinegar, oil and washing soda.

Except for the latter, children can be involved in making up all the potions as an activity and then learn to clean using them, which adds to the fun. The ingredients cost money (although bulk-buying bicarbonate for domestic use is considerably cheaper than for cooking). However, compared to the price of commercial cleaning products, you will save money, be environmentally friendly and have a creative activity as a helpful spin-off.

There are plenty of recipes for cleaning potions on the Poundwise Parenting website.

Make it fun

I have never found cleaning to be motivational so, when cleaning with children, I always put on an interesting audiobook or music so we could dance and dust. Challenges can be set with the music e.g. with the "Flight of the Bumble Bee" (Rimsky-Korsakov), you can say, "Let us see how much we can tidy while the music plays." Then it is a game, not a chore. Another idea is to sing along to music while you clean together.

Don't waste money on cleaning cloths

Old newspapers are better than cloth for cleaning windows. Once you get into the recycling system, you will collect cloth and rags which far exceed your needs. Underwear that children have grown out of, if folded into themselves, make the cutest cleaning pads.

Odd socks make excellent reusable dusters for children and you can wash them easily. Did you know that every house has a sock monster that collects odd ones when you are asleep? Hence, there are usually far more socks than anyone can use.

Establish cleaning as a group activity

Involve children in any household chore from the outset. Do not establish the model that only an adult cleans or tidies. Young children enjoy helping to unload the dishwasher and sort things out. They love sweeping and using a dustpan and brush.

The secret is to work together, while talking and playing language games. Older children can be taught to iron, along with a wide range of cleaning activities.

Clean each other's mess

One game to get bedrooms sorted is to swap the room you clean or tidy. No one likes sorting out their mess, but it seems okay if you sort out someone else's. If you are a single parent, why don't you ask your child to clean your room while you sort theirs rather than let them watch TV? You need to give them the right message.

Confessions of my "Phone-a-cleaner" game

With my youngest two children, I occasionally found that there was a conflict as they needed to be occupied and I needed to clean the house. I resolved this by playing the "Phone-a-cleaner" game.

I pretended that I was a cleaner. I would tell my daughter that I had a phone call from the agency and then I would make a fake call to her and ask her if she could come and help me for a couple of hours.

This daughter, who admittedly loved role play and had an excellent imagination, would rush to the door with her coat on. I pretended to open it and then we would walk around, surveying what needed to be done. After half an hour, we would have the cleaner's snack break and she would tell me about her family. It was so precious and such fun.

We chose music to put on in our pretend customer's house and sang as we cleaned the rooms. It sounds crazy when written down like this, but all I can say is that it worked a dream. The house got cleaned and we had a brilliant time together.

You could spot her sorting out her feelings whenever she talked about her family.

GOING OUT

19

Jumble sales and boot sales

Make sure you get to a jumble sale or boot sale

We live in a consumer culture and some people buy items that they never use. You may even be one of them.

They are not struggling with a budget. They have become accustomed to buying anything for their children to keep up with the latest trends. These people don't know what to do with the surplus goods they have bought (many are still in their original wrappers), so they need to declutter. They send all their cast-offs to jumble sales or sell them at a boot sale. These are the goods you need to track down and buy.

Jumble sales and boot sales are essential when you are on a budget. If you have never visited them, now is the chance to make a remarkable discovery. At the very least, they are purposeful activities and children feel they have been on an outing.

Young people are becoming increasingly aware of environmental concerns and sustainability, and it is fashionable to have second-hand items. Encourage your children, that they are the ultimate in recycling and great for sustainability.

Craft sales are not the same. People are selling items they have made so, understandably, they can be expensive. If you see a craft sale, it could be helpful to wander around and collect inspirational ideas.

Basic Guidelines

Plan it with your children so they feel they are helping to find a bargain.

Find out from the local newspaper or the internet when and where the sales are happening. Ask around for which ones are the best if there is a choice, as they vary in quality and you need to be discerning to get the best bargains.

Tips:

- Go armed with plenty of bags (backpacks are the best).

- Take your own drinks and snacks as it will be counterproductive to buy food.

- Do not wear your best clothes. People always charge more if you look rich.

- Discourage your children from entering tombolas or lucky dips, as they give a poor return.

- If your child wants to buy something, encourage them to barter, as they usually get the best bargains.

- Focus on private cars as these are often individual sellers. Vans often belong to dealers who sell goods they have picked up and are trying to make a living.

- Look for stalls where things have yet to be touched as they often have the best bargains.

The skills you hope to develop in your children will last them for life. You can pride yourself on the fact that you are developing an entrepreneurial spirit in them. Go to the sales with a positive attitude and use the tips I am offering to get the most out of the experience.

Best time to go to a sale

The secret of success for a jumble sale or boot sale is to either arrive at the beginning or near the end. There will be excellent bargains at the beginning and the most fantastic choice. If you want to buy excellent quality toys or resources, this is the time to go, but this will also be when things are most expensive (relatively speaking). Sellers are trying to make money and can be over-optimistic about the value of their goods at the outset, so be careful.

The other time to go to a jumble sale or boot sale is at the end, when a sense of desperation pervades. People will sell you anything for the lowest price rather than repack it and take it home. If you want to make a trip of it and get the best of both worlds, go early and stay as long as possible, but this might be more difficult with young children. You can turn up and go around at the beginning, buy something you could play with outdoors and then go to the edge of the field and let the children play with what you have just bought. Then go back at the end and pick up the bargains.

A boot sale has the added advantage of piles of things left in the field at the end because people don't want to pack them back into their cars. Get to these before the professional cleaners. They are free pickings.

With experience, you will become adept at this. Don't panic at the first sale. You will probably be doing many more in the future.

Games to play

I used to play various games with my children at jumble sales and boot sales.

Give each child an amount you can afford e.g. £1 and then set a time limit. Make your own version of "Bargain Hunt" and set a challenge from the list below.

Challenges

- buy the most goods for that amount of money

- buy something which would be the best fun to play with indoors or outdoors

- buy the best present for someone (name a person)

- buy the smallest thing that you would play with or use

With older children, you can give them more money and get them to buy goods that they think are the best to resell later. Then promise that they can keep any profit they make.

If you have another adult with you, splitting into teams always makes things livelier. If it is just you and a child, you can buy each other a gift you think the other would like. Be prepared to receive something you aren't that keen on.

> ## My Experience
>
> When we challenged our children to buy the most with their money, one of them always interpreted this to mean oversized goods and would buy the largest, ghastliest soft toy imaginable.
>
> Another child would interpret this to mean the most objects and she would come out with armloads.
>
> Yet another would interpret this to mean the goods that you most want. That child would spend endless time wandering up and down, ensuring she bought what she wanted.

Interestingly, the different characters of your children will come out here, although it doesn't matter how they interpret the task. You will have at least one hour when motivated children spend a small amount of money and enjoy themselves. They will develop their social skills and learn about buying and selling.

Consider selling your own things

Another option is to sell your goods at a boot sale. This teaches children about communication as they will meet a lot of people. Even if they are young, they will be watching you. If they have their own things to sell, let them keep the money as they will then learn to sell well.

Older children can be encouraged to use any money they make to buy goods that they think would make a profit on eBay or Vinted. They don't need to make a lot of money, but they will learn a lot by doing the activity.

Stock up

You will be amazed how many expensive items will be on sale at boot and jumble sales. You can often pick up fantastic bargains for Christmas and birthdays, but it requires planning. If they are for your children, take black plastic sacks to hide the items.

Ensure that these presents are logged in a notebook or you will forget what you have. We always spent the same amount of money on each child but, by savvy shopping, they had some fantastic gifts.

I never felt we were short of cash. It was a challenge to be enjoyed.

Be ready for embarrassment

A warning is needed here, as these games will not be without their embarrassing moments. Doubtless, your offspring will produce their own toe-curling behaviour at times.

My Experience

The child I mentioned who interpreted the task as the most objects, once went into a jumble sale in the early 80s, aged seven, with 20 pence. She came out with four carrier bags, full of incredible toys. She was the obvious winner of the challenge.

We quizzed her on how she had managed to get so much decent stuff for only 20p. She looked a little embarrassed and explained that she had shown her smallest coin to the seller, put on her most pitiful face and asked, "Will I get change if I give this to you?"

People felt sorry for her and sold her everything for a penny, believing that she did not know the value of money and was undoubtedly not very bright.

JUMBLE SALES

These are usually organised by people who want to raise money for a good cause, so what you spend goes to charity. This adds to the "feel good factor" for the children. They are usually kind people and motivated to get rid of everything.

An added benefit is that jumble sales are generally good sources of cheap cakes, tea and squash. At the end of the day, your children will have had a productive time for under a tenner.

You can find a lot of goodies to amuse them for endless hours. If you are lucky, you might also have a few Christmas and birthday presents to hide away.

Don't panic if your children buy too many things. They can play with them for a while, and then you can donate them to a charity shop and let others have fun.

This is recycling at its best.

Buy toys for fun

Whilst the children are happily engaged in their quest, you can buy some excellent toys and activities with fun value. Typically, parents look for play value where the children get educational input from a game or toy. When buying from a jumble sale or boot sale, aim to buy toys or games which will provide fun.

You would probably avoid buying a water gun, but this is the time to buy one, or even two. Water is free (time to empty the rainwater butt) and you can have lots of fun with the children in the garden.

You could buy an old tent to put in the garden for a few days. This will lead to lots more activities e.g. a picnic tastes better in a tent and a story being read while squashed up together is much more fun.

The possibilities are endless. It is up to you to look for ideas as you walk around.

Christmas Past

I remember a jumble sale run by a school where I was a supply teacher. I gave five of my children a small amount of money and let them loose. It was November, and they were intent on buying their entire stock of Christmas presents.

When we returned, I saw their excitement as they furtively hid their gifts. I smiled, thinking I had done an excellent job.

On Christmas morning, I was given an enormous pile of ghastly objects. For each one, I had to appear thrilled (as only parents know how) and make each child think their gift was terrific. I was puzzled at the weird and jumbled collection. One of the children could not last without telling me the source of their gifts.

"It came from the school jumble sale, and we knew you wanted it."

"How did you know what I wanted?" I quizzed.

"Well, the lady asked us if we had a penny, and then she showed us your presents and said that you had told her they were the things you wanted, and we could have them for only a penny. Isn't that amazing?"

That was how I discovered that the school staff had offloaded unsaleable junk on my gullible offspring. When I returned to school in January, their delight knew no limits when they heard that their trick had succeeded. It was one of the best jokes I have ever had played on me. It gave me pleasure to think that the children knew I would be happy with the best bargains of a jumble sale. At least they wanted me to be happy. I kept all the items for a decent length of time before surreptitiously offloading them at the next jumble sale.

Online ways to buy second-hand

With the increase of online shopping, second-hand bargains can be found on sites such as Freegle, where unwanted items are given away. It has the advantage that you can create a post if you want a specific item.

There are many community groups on Facebook with selling pages. These are often local and can be a good way of picking up a bargain as well as meeting and networking with like-minded people.

If you search carefully, you can also get fantastic bargains on other sites, such as eBay and Vinted.

20

Travelling

Games for trains, cars and waiting rooms

You will probably travel somewhere with your children in a car, bus or train. Try to maximise the time so that they remember it as a great experience.

When we travelled, we played endless games and each child had their favourite. One always wanted to plan a successful bank raid and relished that he had my undivided attention to explain it to me on a train.

We played word games, guessing games, and number games endlessly. I don't see why children should be expected to sit still and behave. Children spend a lot of time in queues, in doctors' waiting rooms, on journeys, etc and these be fertile teaching times. You are stuck there anyway so, instead of resenting it, turn it into fun. The children often develop ideas for games, and someone sitting near them will join in if you are lucky.

Get as much as you can from the journey

Make sure the children take in as much of the scenery as they can. Talk with them, rather than being on your phone. Enjoy the ride and gain as much as possible.

Your family will soon find which games they enjoy the most, and this will depend on their characters and ages.

Our favourite games

I spy

Someone chooses something they can see and then says the letter it begins with. Traditionally, you say, "I spy with my little eye, something beginning with…"

The others have to guess it. The one who gets it right chooses the next object. This can be played with younger children by saying, for example, "I spy with my little eye, something blue," or "I spy with my little eye, something that is a circle."

Twenty questions

Someone chooses an object, and the others have to guess what it is, but they can only ask twenty questions. The answer can only be "yes" or "no" and a guess counts as a question.

My Experience

On one memorable occasion, we were on a long underground journey, playing "I spy". Commuters were sitting, pretending not to be listening.

Towards the journey's end, my daughter said she spied something beginning with R. We spent ages guessing.

"Are you sure you have the right letter?" I asked, and she assured me she did.

As the train approached the station, I knew that I had to resolve the issue for the ten or so city workers who were pretending to be disinterested, so I said, "I give in."

"It's wrinkles, Mummy. They are by the side of your eyes," she announced gleefully.

Without exception, the smiles on the faces of the commuters revealed that they had been listening, and I hastily exited the train, laughing my head off and blushing.

Alphabet game

Choose a theme and then find a word for every letter of the alphabet for that theme. Example: Animals could be aardvark, bear, chimpanzee, deer, etc.

Work together as a family, and you can set a time limit to make it more fun.

Coloured cars or lorries

Each child chooses a colour and they start to count the cars or lorries in their chosen colour. Select a number and see which child reaches it first.

Predict the number

This is similar to the game above but, for this, how many of a specific vehicle will you see in a pre-agreed length of time as a family? For example, "How many caravans do you think we will see in ten minutes?" The game starts once you have written everyone's guess.

Making up stories

One child starts with a sentence, then the next child adds another sentence to continue creating a story. Go around each member of the family, as often as you can, until the story loses sense.

I am thinking of a number

Someone thinks of a number. The others have to ask whether it is higher or lower than a number they suggest and then work out the number the person is thinking of by the process of elimination. The number of questions and guesses is the score.

With older children, you can play this with high numbers but, with young children, stick to numbers under ten.

I went to a shop and I bought ...

Someone starts with, "I went to the shop and I bought ..." and adds an item. The next child has to say, "I went to the shop, and I bought ..." then says the first person's choice and then adds their own. This goes on, and the game is to see how many objects the children can remember in sequence.

Alternatively, other starting sentences could be:

- I went to the zoo/farm/house and I saw ...

- I went to the party and I ate ...

Backpacks

Make sure that every child (from a young age) has a backpack. I have always been amused when, watching parents with carrier bags hanging off their arms and the pushchair, while the children skip along carrying nothing. Having a backpack means that children can learn to sort themselves out and not have to ask you for everything.

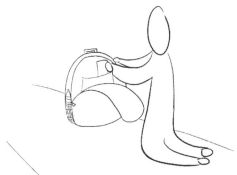

Before you travel, make sure that all essentials are in there. You will save money if you take as many drinks as possible. Give each child a water bottle, which you can usually refill for free. Encourage them to pack necessary things to avoid boredom. This was our approach when we took our children on long car journeys and the first one who said they were bored lost the game.

Download stories to listen to while you travel. It is fun if you have a book to listen to every time you get in the car.

Buy from supermarkets, not cafés

If it is a special occasion and you want more than water, take a large bottle and reusable plastic cups, as this is cheaper than buying individual bottles. You can buy another large bottle from a supermarket when you are out. Label the cups so that they can be reused. Take a knife (not a sharp one) to cut food from supermarkets, such as a cake. This is cheaper than buying them individually.

Be prepared

It is also helpful to have extra things in your bag, particularly if it is a long journey. I would always take some toilet roll, plastic bags for rubbish (and any disaster), wet wipes and water in my backpack. Keep a box of useful things at home to take on a journey, such as:

- a pack of cards (provides endless games)

- notepads

- pencils

- self-contained games (no tiny pieces to lose)

- books

- a small ball or frisbee (these can be used for energetic activities when you have a stop. Children are more inclined to run around with something to throw)

- water and snacks for each child in their backpack (they can then choose when to eat and drink)

My Experience

One of our children would eat their food, almost before we had left our home street. Another child always wanted to be the last to finish so they could boast that they had some left.

21

Shopping for food

Shopping is a crucial area where a tight budget can increase tensions significantly. The children can be demanding and not understand the situation, and it can end up as a bleak experience with you constantly reminding everyone that you can't afford it. Your stress levels are likely to be high so be aware that the only thing you can change is the way you approach it.

Make shopping an outing

Shopping is often an interesting outing for children. I appreciate that you are under stress because of the rising costs, but what you do with the children doesn't have to cost any more. Shops are minefields but the secret is to get them involved in playing a game with you.

If you can change from thinking that shopping is the worst activity to do with children to being fun, it will transform things.

Have a plan before you shop

Since supermarkets are designed to make you spend money, do not be surprised if your children throw a temper tantrum because they want something. It might not be acceptable, but it is understandable. When you don't have much money, it is difficult to watch others fill their trolleys with goods you wished you could afford. For years, I have adopted a strict shopping policy. Leave home with a shopping list of essential items and a clear budget. Otherwise, you will buy things you don't need.

If you don't have a lot of money, you will need every ounce of creativity to feed your children as healthily as possible.

Involve the children

For younger children, you can write a short list of three or four things you want to buy and draw pictures to match them. This will give them a focus.

As they get older, they could write the list. Let children who enjoy maths add things up as they go along by giving them a calculator or your phone.

The recent addition of scanners can be an advantage because you know how much you are spending. Give an older child the scanner and make them responsible for getting it all within budget.

Stick to your budget

Avoid anything going into the trolley that you can't afford.

If you only have £5 for the day, make sure everyone knows this at the outset. This is where cash is much easier for the children to understand the system. If you use your card, a child thinks it is a bottomless pit. As we have emerged from Covid, the days when we regularly used cash have long gone.

If you are determined, you can have money up to your limit, and let the child watch it going down as an excellent maths activity, and then pay for it on a card if you have to. This idea might work with younger children, but you could probably do it as a paper exercise for older ones.

Teaching your children to shop wisely is an invaluable life lesson, so don't feel bad. Calling it a challenge helps to create the idea of a game.

My Experience

I know of a mother who had no money in her account and was fed up with her 13-year-old constantly moaning that she would not buy things. She went with the child to the cash machine with the promise that she could take out as much as she wanted, and the mother promised to spend it in the shops. Of course, it didn't take long for the child to discover that there wasn't any money in the account!

A bit harsh, I guess, and it goes against not trying to burden children with the anxiety surrounding the financial crisis but may be worth considering in desperate situations.

If the children know the budget limit, it should eliminate their requests for chocolate and cakes and to be taken to a café. If you have money to spare, then clearly state how much the treat money is, then create a game where everyone has to agree on a treat with that amount.

Tip:

Buy treats in supermarkets rather than small shops

It is significantly cheaper to buy a box of ice creams from the frozen dessert range in a supermarket than to buy them individually in a shopping centre, especially if you have a large family. If you only have one or two children, it can still be cheaper to buy a pack of 6 and it is fun to give away spares to strangers (see Chapter 15: Angels and acts of random kindness).

You can also join the Facebook pages of like-minded parents and get some fabulous ideas instead of thinking you have to come up with everything yourself (see Poundwise Parenting website for links).

Look for budget lines in every shop

Some shops, such as Iceland, offer a range of £1 items. They claim they are running at a loss with these products, so make sure you buy them. Every major supermarket runs a bargain range. Find out which ones are in your store, then check the ingredients and prices with your children to see if they are good value. If you see yourselves as jointly trying to beat the shop, you take the emphasis off your lack of money.

Spot the bargains

Every supermarket has a system for cutting the price of goods approaching their sell-by date. The later in the day, the lower the prices although you do not save anything if you aren't going to eat it. The excitement of seeing something for only 10p will soon disappear if you bin the item the next day.

I look for things that we will eat and can be frozen. The canny shopper soon learns the best time for their supermarket, and I have taken my children out on special trips then to see if we can catch some bargains.

Ensure the reductions are good enough to warrant the short shelf life. An alternative approach is to decide that evening's meal based on what is reduced. This can give some exciting results.

Look at the week's Buy One Get One Free (BOGOF) or 3 for 2 offers, and the manager's specials. Check if they are worth buying but beware, as they are not always the best value. These products are usually positioned at the end of the aisles to attract your attention, so take them to similar ones and compare the value. Ask the children, "Are we being tricked?" Always talk to them about what is worth getting and what isn't. They will need this skill for the rest of their lives.

My Experience

I remember an embarrassing occasion when I had hit a perfect time for reductions and managed to fill my trolley with bargains.

I turned to get something off the shelf and, when I looked back, a couple were sorting through my trolley, mistakenly thinking it was the bargain trolley for all customers. I was horrified at the thought of all my reductions being taken by someone else, and they were not happy that I had got there before them.

It was one of my grimmer moments as they marched away, muttering.

Always look for sell-by dates and get food from the back of the shelf with a longer shelf life. Older children enjoy this game, although it is less popular in supermarkets. Instead of just grabbing the first loaf of bread at the front, get the freshest one.

Our children learned early to compare prices using the "per 100g" information on the tickets. If you look closely, many of the apparent bargain family-size things are not the cheapest. You can play a "Points game" where you see if you can beat the supermarket five times to get the best deal during one shopping session.

Play games

Even if you are operating the trolley, you can give most children a basket, and some stores have mini trolleys. Depending on their age, they can sort out some of the shopping as they get the hang of it e.g. you can say to an older child, "We need cornflakes. Bring me back the box that you think is the best value today. If you aren't sure, pick two finalists, and then we can decide which is the winner."

This activity also gives the child plenty of exercise while you get the rest of the shopping done.

My Experience

When my children were younger, I used to take the youngest ones to go shopping. We needed ten loaves of bread a week and the children loaded the trolley with two loaves at a time whilst reciting, "One, two, buckle my shoe, three, four, knock at the door."

When we bought eggs, we sang, "Chick, chick, chick, chicken, lay a little egg for me." I am sure people thought we were crazy, but it made a shopping trip fun.

Consider bigger issues

As a family, you could consider the wider ethical issues of eating less meat or cutting it out altogether. This can be a way of extending your budget and helping the environment.

The world has changed considerably in the last few years, and now there is plenty of dietary information on packaging. Teach your children about this and include it when deciding what is, and isn't, good value. Play a game and try to avoid foods with red indicators on the traffic light system.

Get children involved with meal planning and shopping

A fun challenge is to set a budget for one meal, one day's shopping, or even meals for a whole week, and ask the children to plan the menus and do the shopping.

The children may have to visit a few shops, market stalls etc, to achieve it within the budget limit. As our children got older and moaned about what they weren't allowed, we gave them a turn to do the shopping within the weekly food budget. They only did it once but it cut down the gripes.

Another game with older children is for them to each have a trolley, split the list, and then compete to see who gets everything on their list first.

Sometimes it's best to go on your own

Having said all this, you need to be realistic as there will be times when all this effort seems too much and you want to shop on your own and leave the children with someone else or when they are at school. Enjoy.

22

Online shopping

Many people mistakenly think that online shopping is not a good idea if you are short of money, but it can be a valuable tool to help you save money.

Easier to keep to a budget online

One of the most significant advantages of online shopping is that you can stick to a budget.

Nothing is more embarrassing than getting to a physical checkout and realising that you have exceeded your budget. Then, often with a long queue waiting, it is awful deciding which items you will ask them to take back.

It is much easier to remove things from your trolley in a virtual world where you can put things in and out of your trolley, and no one knows.

Easier to compare prices online

Another massive advantage of online shopping is that it is much easier to compare prices. This is difficult when you have children with you and it is more tempting to take the offers and not check that they are cheaper. Supermarket layouts are designed to lure you into buying things you don't want, with items strategically placed to entice you.

Try the experiment of buying cheese online. It is easy to compare how much everything is per 100g whereas, in the shop, the price per 100g is easily missed. You can quickly spot the best value online.

Find ways to reduce delivery costs

The delivery charge is one of the problems with internet shopping. However, the competition is fierce between supermarkets and most will offer a cheaper deal if you are prepared to have a longer window for delivery or have food delivered at less sociable hours. It is easy to shop from the comfort of your settee and the idea of someone else running around the shop, picking everything up and bringing it to your door, does make it rather attractive. When working out your budget, the delivery cost is usually less than the bus fare or petrol you would have spent.

Consider "Click and Collect" as a free alternative, where you place the order online and then collect it from the store. This saves time and it means that you won't overspend. Although don't forget to factor in the petrol cost.

One idea is for a group to shop together, split the delivery cost and meet up when it is delivered. You will all have saved time. It also gives you a chance to buy offers and split them. You can buy larger sizes and decant them but check your prices because bigger isn't necessarily cheaper.

Most supermarkets do an annual delivery pass, which gives unlimited deliveries and is more affordable if you can manage the initial outlay. The downside is that they only deliver to one address, so it would probably work better if you live close together.

Some supermarkets allow you to book a regular slot. If you hate shopping in-store, this is a bonus. You can stick to your budget and it can be an easy way to have the basics delivered. Retailers work hard to create a cheaper range of food to help those on a budget, but people may be embarrassed to put this range in their trolley in front of everyone else (although they should be proud). When it is delivered, only the delivery driver knows what you have chosen.

Easier to find healthy options online

When money is tight, it can be tough to feed your children healthily. An advantage of online shopping is that you can click on an item and scroll down to see the contents. It is easier to make healthier choices when you have time to look at this. If you have someone in your family with allergies, it is easier to check the contents of everything you buy.

Online shopping saves time

Although it is a time-saver, online shopping isn't a substitute for shopping with your children. There is a lot to be enjoyed and learned by taking them with you, but you can do this at different times.

Online shopping as a game

A beneficial and fun activity with older children is for them to shop online with you and discuss food choices without being in the shop. You can play a game like "You only have £20 and the person you are shopping for is allergic to milk. Can you shop for the weekend?" This could be made into a competition.

Of course, you can always do your own online shopping with your child. This is a wonderful way to teach them the value of money and show them how to make difficult choices.

Online shopping can get quicker every time

All supermarkets have a list of favourites and save every order you place so that you can do your shopping quickly on future occasions. Save your shopping under different headings to create lists. Then when you click a list, this is added to your online basket. Be careful that new offers come on and prices change, so ordering the identical thing the following week may not be the cheapest.

Another recent trend is that many larger supermarkets have realised that their prices are being beaten by shops like Aldi, so they offer to price-match lots of items. Since Aldi and Lidl have an expensive delivery system, you can get the best of both worlds.

Find budget recipes

The majority of supermarkets also provide online recipes which include value options. Sainsbury's has a range called "Feed your family for a fiver" where you can pick up some ideas. It is easy to click on the ingredients and add them to your trolley.

Check out the offers

Another useful tab is the "Offers" which is universal. It is so much easier to sort out which offers are worth having. Asda's suggestions are in price order, so it is possible to look for offers under £1, etc. If you are shopping with the children and the money is tight, if you have £1 left, you could let them choose something from the list. Different supermarkets organise things in various ways.

Online shopping allows for last-minute changes

This is an advantage of internet shopping as you can change your order as late as the night before delivery, so you can add things at the last minute and not go to expensive small local shops. Also, if your plans change, as they often do with children, you don't have to shop at the last minute.

Fully use incentive schemes

Some shops offer a points scheme, which can be exchanged for more than the monetary value of experiences and offers, offering excellent value.

Maximise first shop offers

Many supermarkets offer customers an introductory offer. If you are savvy, you can have a "first shop" with all of them before selecting the one which offers the best value.

Use apps to save money and avoid waste

It is worth investigating some of the online apps that help minimise food wastage (see the Poundwise Parenting website for the latest list). An example is "Too Good to Go" which offers heavily reduced food local to you at the end of the day from bakeries, cafés, shops and restaurants.

23

Museums and art galleries

Most places have a museum which is usually cheap, if not free. You may have had bad experiences visiting museums as a child but things have changed considerably. Most museums increasingly use technology, and many offer a wonderfully interactive experience and a great outing.

Go online before the trip

If planning a trip to a museum, you can look online so that you know what to expect. If you are motivated, you could draw pictures of items and ask your children to tick them off when seen.

Alternatively, you can take screenshots and ask if they can find the pictures. You can look at the website with older children so that they can choose what they want to look at.

Eat and drink before you go

Ensure everyone has had plenty to eat and drink before you start a museum or gallery visit. Hungry and thirsty children become grumpy and ask how much longer until they can eat.

Make sure it is fun

Always ask what is available at the outset, as many museums have trail sheets, puzzles and games. Scan them before passing them to the children to ensure that they are appropriate and won't make the trip boring. It is easy to get obsessed with filling in answers on a sheet and not focusing on what interests the child. Some museums have their sheets so you can check and print them before you leave.

Be clear about the rules

Ensure the children are clear about appropriate behaviour in museums or art galleries, otherwise, it will become a nightmare. The most important rule is "No touching" which must be observed or you will be asked to leave.

Have a plan for the children if they get lost. Our children knew to go to a security guard or to stay where they were, and we would come back for them. They knew not to go anywhere with anyone else. I found it challenging to get the balance between wanting to let my children be interested and move around and not boring them by making them watch what I thought was necessary. It is easy to lose a child as they tend to wander off, with such a wide range of things to look at. Ensure your mobile phone number is written on paper in each child's pocket.

Don't stay too long

Let the children go at their own speed. You may need to introduce challenges and ask questions to prevent them from rushing around at top speed. However, do not expect to stay too long at a museum or gallery.

If the children aren't interested and none of the following games help, move on somewhere else. Another idea is to take a ball or frisbee with you, do half an hour, go outside, play a game, and then go back in.

Make it fun with creative suggestions

Generally, you can make even the dullest place enjoyable by introducing a personal element. In a museum, I would go into each section and ask the children, "If you could take one thing home, what would you take and why?"

Ideally, your children are fascinated with history or artistic value, but even if they are looking at something, you have had some success.

My Experience

One of my most embarrassing moments was when I took the children to Stonehenge. We had joined the National Trust for a year and had to visit as many places as possible to get our money's worth.

I had done all the educational stuff and my 7-year-old asked to go to the shop. I figured he might as well and thought he could learn something.

When I joined him shortly later, I was horrified to find him lying on the floor with his hand under one of the gondolas.

"What are you doing?" I asked.

"Oh, Mum," came the embarrassingly loud reply, "people have dropped their coins in this shop, and they have fallen under here. I am getting them out so I can buy something."

Yes, I did make him retrieve them and give them in, much to his fury.

Get the children to make it more interesting

A game you can play is to ask each child to make up a question about the museum. Then you all look around the displays to find the answers. This means that the children will look at most of the exhibits.

Take your own art materials

Take colouring pencils/crayons and paper/notebooks so that each child can draw their favourite exhibit. Never buy pencils or crayons from a museum or art gallery, as they are expensive.

Creative questions make it more rewarding

In museums, ask the children to find the exhibit that scares or makes them laugh the most.

In art galleries, each picks the painting they would choose to have at home. Another slant is to ask which exhibit or painting they like least.

Or choose a theme and see how many pictures you can find with that theme e.g. fruit, food, water, children, etc. A child who is interested in art or history won't need these games, but some will benefit from having a focus.

As you look at a picture, ask questions to make it come alive, such as:

- What might have happened before the picture was painted?

- What is the person thinking?

- What is behind one of the objects in the painting?

- What do you think will happen next?

- How does this picture make you feel?

- What does the artist want you to look at first?

- Which painting has the most violence?

These questions will keep some less motivated children looking.

The children can come up with their own challenges and, once they get into it, all trips are fun.

I also use this approach when stuck in a large, expensive shop. I ask the children to spot what they think is the most dreadful item in the shop. A word of warning here, ask them to show you discreetly and certainly not when someone is buying it, as has happened to me.

Involve the staff

Whenever possible, talk to the security staff. It makes trips more exciting and stretches them out. Staff are often keen to tell you extra bits and, if you ask them interesting questions, you will gain extra information. If your children aren't keen to ask questions, set an example and ask them yourself.

The shop

There is always a shop at the end of every trip and you need a strategy to get through it without spending a lot. These shops are full of expensive products and must be avoided when on a budget. Sometimes, however, they are unavoidable as they are between you and the exit.

The cheapest method, if you have any money, is to let the children choose a postcard of their favourite exhibit or picture. This activity lasts at least 20 minutes and costs about 70p. Stick to only one picture each or the trip will become expensive. Ensure each child pays separately, so that they get their own bag, although you might not be popular with the sales assistant.

Annual memberships can be an investment

Depending on where you live, it might be worth investing in an annual National Trust or Heritage ticket membership (English Heritage, Heritage Trust Network Northern Ireland, Cadw in Wales, and Historic Scotland). They all sell family tickets.

If someone wants to buy you something for Christmas, consider asking for money towards an annual membership. We had these on alternate years and they gave us several free days out, and we visited the same place more than once if the children particularly liked it. The secret to a positive trip is not to spend too long in any room.

They always have fantastic gardens and many have dressing-up and appropriate multi-sensory activities to help children learn. I have never found any member of staff who was unwilling to talk to children and encourage them in their learning.

There are often interesting trails in the garden and play areas, and each place makes a massive effort at Christmas.

You must take food and drink, as their cafés are expensive.

BOLD APPROACH TO HOLIDAYS

24

House exchange

Share everything, and I mean everything

By now, you will have realised that to make it through on a tight budget, you will need to share everything you have. The single most valuable commodity is your house. I must warn you that this takes a lot of brain rearranging. On a budget, renting anywhere for a holiday is impossible so you need to start using where you live. I realise this may be impossible for some people, so read the next chapter on Staycation.

The principle is simple. You swap houses with a family like yours who are also strapped for cash. We discovered this in the summer when we had three children under four and no money for anything, certainly not a holiday. I was incredibly nervous the first time but so desperate to get away and have a change of scenery that I did it, and then I was hooked.

Over fourteen years, we did twenty-six house exchanges, mainly in the UK, but six were in Holland and six were in Ireland.

Your home is invaluable to someone else

You might not find where you live inspirational but, for someone else, it is a fantastic place. Some of our best holidays were in areas that may not be considered holiday destinations, but we were always energised by different surroundings.

You can become part of a new community

One of the best parts is that because you are in someone else's house, you become part of their community, and we discovered we had visits from the other people's friends. We were invited to barbeques and our children were often asked to play with friends of the children who lived there.

Swap with a similar-sized family

Anyone can join. A single parent with one child in a small flat can swap with a similar-sized family, and a large family with a huge house can also exchange holidays. It is essential to swap similar setups as the house and contents will then be suitable for your family.

There will be more space than in a caravan or a tent and a great advantage is that there will probably be a washing machine, a freezer and a television.

If you think about it, your house would be locked up while you are away if you do not swap, so it makes sense to save money by using this resource.

How do I find someone to exchange with?

There are numerous schemes which charge a small administrative fee to join.

Why don't you suggest an initial exchange with friends who live at a distance from you? This would help you to try out the pitfalls and see if you could cope with swapping with strangers.

Set up your own scheme within an interest group

The current economic climate may cause the formation of new house exchange schemes. If you belong to any interest groups, setting up your own scheme should be possible as the principle is relatively simple.

Offer to produce a list of the houses people have to swap and what they would like, then charge them a nominal fee for the list when compiled.

From the list, they can decide who might fit their criteria and contact the owner to arrange a swap. You are trying to match like-minded people but have no responsibility for any exchange made.

What about pets?

You must clearly state if you have pets, and which pets you would accept in your house, if any. If that is clear at the outset, swaps will be made with compatible people. An advantage of a house exchange is that, by agreement, you can feed each other's animals and water each other's plants.

My Experience

We sometimes left our chickens as our swap families were happy to feed them and have the eggs in exchange.

We once arrived at a house and found two 3-week-old kittens that the owners had forgotten to mention. That was interesting.

Our children were thrilled and it added to their holiday experience.

Advantages

There are considerable advantages to the scheme, as we discovered. Primarily, once you have subscribed, there are no further accommodation charges. Secondly, you can stay in a house/flat/bungalow which is full of all the correct equipment and more useful items than would be found in a rental property.

Tip:

Only swap with someone who has children in a similar age group to yours. There will then be age-suitable books, activities and toys so you only have to take minimal belongings.

What if other people can't be trusted?

You may say that you could not do what we were doing as you may not trust other people. However, if you challenge your thinking; you only need to trust others as much as they need to trust you. You would not abuse the opportunity, so it is unreasonable to presume that others would.

In practice, you will get to know the swap families before the holiday, through phone calls or online face-to-face conversations.

However, there will be horror stories of when things go wrong, so check your house insurance.

Decide your rules

Before the swap, I always phone the family to agree on our house rules.

- Use anything you want and replace it if possible. I will leave a stocked cupboard and the basics in the fridge.

- Use as many herbs, spices, etc as you like.

- Use the house phone for any calls and leave cash for payment. I will leave a list of the charges. (These days, we agree to only use mobile phones.)

- Electricity and gas are on a like-for-like basis.

- Use anything in our house, as we will have removed anything we do not want you to touch.

Do an initial shop for each other

When travelling abroad, or with very young children, it can be helpful to agree to do each other's shopping for the first 24 hours. After a long journey, you have everything you need to settle down for a while.

Get your house in order

Nothing will motivate you more to clean your house or force your children to tidy and sort their toys, than the idea of another family living in your space. It is an exciting concept but if this idea repels you, please skip this section.

My Experience

I must admit that the week before a house exchange always made me panic, as I realised what a mess everything was. I went on obsessive labelling and list-writing enterprises before I could swap. I was always scared (even the last time) that others would be disappointed in my house or the area I lived. We don't live anywhere that would be seen as a tourist place, although it is suitable to access other places.

My fears were always unfounded as everyone on this scheme was like-minded and tended to be resourceful and creative and grateful for a holiday.

I have never been a natural camper. What is the point of leaving a comfortable house to be squashed in an expensive caravan or tent? I have yet to discover one with a washing machine and flushable toilet. I prefer to have lots of space and a new area to explore.

My Experience

In twenty-six swaps, we have only had one burnt spatula and a set of bikes that needed servicing after a Dutch family rode them as though they were the old solid Dutch bikes their children were used to.

Without exception, we broke a glass in every house we stayed in, no matter how hard we tried not to. We always had to buy a set of six to replace them, as they could never be matched.

Items to leave in your house

- A list of instructions for any machines they might use (put sticky labels on them for simplicity)

- A collection of leaflets on local resources

- A list of places you take your children that are not typical tourist attractions e.g. the best parks or the best picnic spots

- A list of peculiarities in your house, as it is helpful to know which door needs to be kicked to open, which drawer needs to be lifted to shut, etc.

My Experience

On one house exchange, we woke the first morning to discover that the fridge was not working. We rang the owners, who explained that they had wired it in with the mains cooker switch so when we switched everything off at night, the fridge had gone off too.

Ask your swap family to provide a similar set of items. If you are swapping with a family from another country, ask for any vital information to be written in English.

Arriving at the new house

Before your children are allowed into the house, take photos of every room, so that you can restore them before you leave.

My Experience

We arrived late at night in Holland to find a list on the kitchen table entirely in Dutch. We were scared it might be dangerous if we did something wrong, so we waited until the next day to learn from bilingual neighbours that it was only a set of instructions for operating the washing machine.

Tip:

Put clean bedding on all beds in your house and ask the swap family to strip the beds when they leave. It is easier to wash bedding in your own house on your return and it reduces the luggage. We did take towels for the children to use at the beach.

The penultimate day of the house swap

This day is also a nightmare as you feel you must leave their house in pristine condition. My personal goal was to leave it better than when we entered. I was always scared that people would think I was dirty, so the last 24 hours were a total frenzy. Still, because of the non-existent accommodation charges, it was the best-paid cleaning I could ever have done.

We involved the children in returning everything to how it was when we arrived. This was never popular but it was an essential part of their education.

Tip:

If your host family has cleaners, perhaps they will let you have their number. Paying someone to clean their house when you leave is a wonderful luxury. The advantage of this is that the family will be satisfied with the standard. If you know anyone who would appreciate the job, you can leave their contact number for the family living in your house.

What is gained from a house exchange?

The children gained a lot as they travelled to places we could not normally have afforded. We could go away for longer than if we had accommodation costs. We were very spoilt as we were both teachers and could spend the majority of the school holidays away.

It helped our children to be less selfish, as they learned to make their rooms ready for someone else. They left little notes in their bedrooms before they left, and also for the child whose room they had stayed in.

They had the experience of living elsewhere, and they had our undivided attention as we were together as a family.

One of the most significant advantages is that in someone else's house, even the local park becomes a new place for your children. Taking a picnic just down the street is converted into an outing.

On one exchange, we made a fire and played games around it; something we had never experienced with our children.

My Experience

We swapped for a fortnight with a family with six children in the Lake District. We had a wonderful time but were surprised that everything shut at 5.30 pm. We live in an area with 24-hour supermarkets and a shopping mall that stays open until 10.00 pm.

I was worried that our exchange family would hate the swap as they lived in such a beautiful area. When we spoke afterwards, the mother said it was her best holiday. She had been out shopping every evening with the older children; something she had never done before as she always had her younger ones during the day. She had managed to do her entire Christmas shopping and was thrilled.

You learn a lot just by living in someone else's home.

My Experience

Our first house exchange was with a family in Birmingham, which may not seem like an ideal holiday location. We had no alternative and it was a fantastic time. We looked up everything free and ran out of time to do everything we wanted. I discovered that other families did different things with their children but that overall, everyone is similar.

I learned an interesting thing on that exchange. The house we found ourselves in was a minefield of sewn, crocheted and knitted items. I was horrified as I had never thought to make anything like it for my children, as I had never been good at craftwork. The furthest I ever got was making Clothkit (ready-cut) dresses for my daughters. That house had beautiful hand-crafted cushions in all the children's rooms, toilet rolls with multi-coloured covers, embroidered bookmarks, and crocheted name plaques on the doors. I panicked and considered that my children must be deprived.

After the swap, I confessed how bad I felt and how much I admired this mother. She laughed and said she hadn't even noticed the lack of such things in my house but felt she was a failure as a mother because she had never thought of a dressing-up, art or music box, all of which had kept her children amused for the whole fortnight.

It was a beneficial exchange.

The good news

Just for the record, to reassure you, every house we stayed in had a cupboard stuffed with things that fell out when you opened the door.

No one is good at cleaning everything. Some had clean windows and mirrors, others had dust-free lampshades, some had excellent ovens but grubby drawers, and so on. Everyone had at least one room that needed urgent redecoration and many had a lot more.

Ultimately, none of it mattered as we had a free holiday.

After the house exchange

It is satisfying to know that your efforts have enabled two families to have a brilliant holiday. When you return to your house, everything is usually in the wrong place and it is strange to think that another family has lived in it. However, it doesn't take long to get it back to how you like it and it has been spring-cleaned for at least another year.

We always contacted our families and chatted about their experiences and ours. Sometimes we met them on the return journey so that the children could see who they had swapped with.

If a swap is successful, you can do it again at a different time of year or a few years later.

My Experience

We once swapped with an Irish family and agreed to meet them at the ferry terminal as they were leaving on the boat we were arriving on. This should have been a good idea, but we had been travelling for twelve hours with four young children before we met them, at the start of their journey.

They were very polite and looked immaculate but we looked a shambles by the time we had got off the boat. I am sure they were worried about what would happen to their house.

25

Staycation

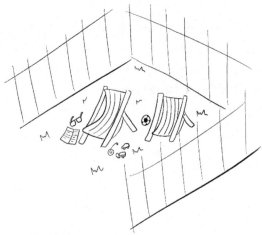

The Urban Dictionary* defines "staycation" in the following ways:

A vacation that is spent at one's home enjoying all that home and one's home environs have to offer.

A vacation spent close to home.

Staying at home during your vacation instead of travelling to a pleasurable destination. This can be caused by high gas prices or just a shortage of money.

*Urban Dictionary Urbandictionary.com

Ironically, "gas" here means petrol, but now takes on a different meaning.

Younger generations have grown up expecting to go on at least one annual overseas vacation and several shorter trips to various locations. The problem is, what can you do when you can't afford it? It is time to consider having a staycation.

This is a relatively new word that has emerged from the economic situation of the last twenty years. Shortage of money is not a recent phenomenon.

It means having to stay home and make the most of the fact that you can't afford to do anything else.

Staycation isn't new

Staycation is, in fact, a return to the practices of about fifty years ago when children spent most of their summer holidays at home, generally with their mothers, whilst their fathers worked.

For people my age, it is not something revolutionary. I was in my mid-forties when I first flew on a plane. We did not have theme parks or computers, and we didn't have mobile phones.

We only had a few toys and books with our siblings to find enjoyment. A few day trips on a train would have been highlights. When we arrived at the beach, we played on the sand and didn't do anything else. I remember the colossal treat of being allowed a donkey ride and our few photographs showed the annual joy.

I do not want you to think it was terrible, as it wasn't. A good thing which came from that was that we became resourceful parents as we had been trained in self-dependence. There will be people whose experiences are entirely different. I am the product of my childhood, which has good and bad parts. The good part is that it never occurred to me that not having money was terrible because we had fantastic fun and were rarely bored.

I don't know how or when things changed. Possibly as a reaction to having little in their childhood, many parents tried to give their children what they considered a better upbringing and did everything in their power to provide them with material things they lacked.

The result is a generation which works hard to offer their children more things, e.g. birthday parties have exploded from a simple event into something costly and often competitive.

We must face reality as we can't afford to keep this up.

Staycations can be life-changing

If taken seriously, a staycation can build a bond with your children and create memories that will be a stronger foundation for their teenage years than any expensive holiday.

Staycations may become the norm as having a holiday at home with plenty of money is easier than a holiday with hardly any. You can take the children out daily, eat expensive meals and spend a fortune.

This chapter addresses the more complex, yet significantly more rewarding, task of staying at home with no more than the usual amount you have to live on, which might not be a lot.

Staycation isn't just staying at home

Make sure to distinguish these ideas from those activities that can be done on a rainy day, although these are useful and could be used to support your staycation. Books can fill spaces when you can't think what to do with your children.

This idea is about changing your mindset towards spending one week or so with your family.

- For every waking moment of your staycation, think about what you can all do that is special, fun and different.

- Look at life and each other from a different perspective.

- Rules are to be changed and, just as everything on holiday is different, so everything about a staycation is changed.

- Roles may need to be reversed, and everyone should be involved at a level appropriate for their age.

- In the same way as you put effort into packing for a holiday, you put time and consideration into working out ideas for a staycation.

Where do you start?

Put the dates of the staycation on the calendar, as you would a holiday.

Take time off from work and, in every respect, act as if you are away. Take a break from anything you do weekly since this is when you will bond and have some fun.

Establish the basic rules

- No one can do what they usually do in their working lives, so no emails, phone calls or texts to or from your workplace.

- Get organised as you would if you were leaving the house.

- Ensure the house is clean and tidy before the staycation begins and don't worry about keeping it spotless during the middle period. Treat it like a holiday rental and let it get messy if needed.

- Plan each day. Maybe each family member can choose what to do each day or part of it. This encourages everyone to listen to each other and try things someone else's way.

- Before the staycation, hide some of the children's toys and books, or collect a new set of toys/books/activities from charity shops and jumble sales (see Chapter 19: Jumble sales and boot sales). The day before the staycation starts, put away most of the current toys and substitute them with the new set. This way, the children all have fresh things to play with, making it more special. (This idea can be helpful even if you aren't doing a staycation). Most children have accrued too many toys and only play with a fraction of them. Keep the ones they constantly play with and swap the rest, but never sort them when the children are around. For some obscure reason, they get upset if anything is packed away. So the secret is to box up half the surplus toys and books and, every six months, do a swap. You will be surprised how much more everything gets played with. It also allows you to throw away anything broken or not played with.

Tip for Special Box
(Not just for Staycations)

I have always felt I could survive anything during the day if my children slept at night. Unfortunately, some of them were lively and woke up too early.

I had to find a creative solution to this problem, so I got a box which I called the special box. After the child had fallen asleep, I would put this at the end of the bed. If they woke up, they were not to leave their room but were encouraged to open the box.

I ensured that it contained suitable toys and books they hadn't seen for ages and also put a drink in it.

The plan worked well. They were happy and did not feel deprived, and I stayed asleep. As you will discover from reading the rest of the book, I found various ways of getting great toys and books from different places. You can swap toys for these boxes with other parents who have the same problem.

Hard work but worth it

Having a proper staycation will be challenging. It is not about keeping the children happy but engaging with them at a more creative level. Having a staycation will guarantee that you learn things about each other, positive and negative, that you would not have had the chance to discover otherwise.

Except for very young children, they must understand what the special staycation time is all about and be included in the new way of doing things. It is not just about parents giving their children a good time. It is for adults to have fun and remember what it was to pretend, imagine, create and enjoy. A staycation may have been forced on you for economic reasons, but it could become an unforgettable life experience. It is entirely up to you.

Anyone can have a staycation. You do not have to be a conventional family and the principles apply just as much for single parents with one child, as for large families.

Having a staycation is a positive choice, not the default option. It is about staying at home and doing lots of creative activities outlined in the rest of the book, for one or two weeks. It is for people who want to put more fun back into the family and those who wish to discover or develop their creativity with their families.

How to make it different practically

It is helpful to set up a theme for the week or each day and think of relevant activities. Once you have the theme, it will kick-start your creativity and you will develop fantastic ideas.

You need to act as if you have no alternative and don't resort to spending money to make it work. Once you get going, you won't need suggestions. Your children will be full of ideas as well.

- Camping day
- Food day
- Making things
- Making a mess
- Orange day (or any colour)
- Circle day (or any shape)
- Outdoors day
- YES day, where (within reason) parents say yes to everything
- Pyjama day

Change everything

- Change your sleeping arrangements. You can all sleep together in one room by moving your bedding, mattresses, etc. You can set up various camps, depending on your type of family.

- Change your timetable. You no longer have to fit into normal getting up or settling down times. There is no school the next day and no one has to go to work, so make the most of it.

- Make a big fuss about breakfast, something like pancakes that you don't usually have time for but are an activity in themselves. Young children can make the batter, older children can cook them, and you have an instant competition with tossing them.

- Change where you eat. Put a tablecloth on the floor. Eat in the garden or the park. Convert one of the rooms into a cave using blankets and eat in there. Do anything to make it more fun.

- Try eating food while you are blindfolded, with the others directing you. Eat out of different containers, use chopsticks, and try feeding each other. Make it like a party. Remember you are on holiday and the usual rules no longer apply.

- Change the family dynamics. Ask the quieter ones to input rather than the one who usually makes the decisions. Value every idea and don't dismiss the ones you think are impossible. Enter the experience with a "can do" attitude, rather than saying it will never work. Start playing with ideas and try things out. It doesn't matter if suggestions don't work. You will always remember trying.

Keep a record

Take lots of photographs of everything you do. At the end of each day, share what you have done to make it less of a random event.

Make an online slide series of the staycation, with a holiday title. Save it as you would if you had gone abroad.

Depending on your family dynamics, you may go different ways and have alternative activities, so your children have special times with each parent (presuming you have the luxury of two). If you are a single parent, find a friend and consider setting up a staycation in one of your houses and doing it jointly. This will only work if you get on well with each other and your kids get on. Discuss the financial implications for the person hosting it and split the costs.

Explore your area

Find places to go. Often we go to a different area on holiday and find lots of enjoyable free activities. Somehow, we become familiar with where we live that we forget there are still great things to do and see.

Before the staycation, discover what things you can find and even if you visit the same place you always go to, you can always make it more interesting by doing treasure hunts, etc (see Chapter 8: Challenges).

During the school holidays, there are usually lots of local activities advertised online and in local newspapers and magazines.

A staycation is a green option

The recession may have forced us to think about a staycation but, long after the recession is over, it will remain a greener alternative to more conventional holidays.

As you read this book, you will discover that it recommends recycling materials rather than using more of the earth's limited resources. A staycation is the most environmentally friendly holiday anyone could have. There is no travelling to get to your destination, which significantly saves carbon emissions. The underlying ethic of sharing and pooling resources has to be one we want to instil in our children and a staycation gives parents a chance to model this behaviour.

A staycation is about celebrating and enjoying the environment that you are in, rather than seeking out new places to enjoy.

Conclusion

Dear Reader,

Thank you for reading this book and letting me share some of my memories and ideas. I don't know where you are on your parenting journey or how hard you are struggling with your budget. What happens now is down to you. Please use this book as your springboard to a positive future. I hope you will become part of the Poundwise Parenting group and work together to improve it for us all.

Don't strive to be the best parent; it is enough to do the best you can.

Your children are unlikely to be grateful, so let me say a huge "thank you" on their behalf until they fully appreciate you.

You are amazing, and I wish you all the best.

Ruth Wise

Acknowledgements

I would like to thank my wonderful husband and children for their encouragement and support in the production of this book. They know the part they have each played in putting the fun into dysfunctional. I love them all to the moon and back.

This book would not have been written if I had not joined the 'Write That Book' course, led by the inspirational Michael Heppell. It has proved to be a life-changing experience and I greatly appreciate the fantastic support of each member of my mentor group: Charmaine, Jane, Mark, Debra, Erika, Sam, Lis, Elaine and Penelope.

Georgia Hutchinson's wonderful illustrations have brought my book to life. Despite being young in years, the flair of her unique style illustrates maturity and great vision.

Thanks go to the gifted Christine Beech for her thorough and insightful editing which has transformed my rambling text.

I greatly appreciate Matt Bird, who is the most amazing typesetter and went far beyond his remit with his hard work and support to give the book its shape and style.

I am grateful to the incredible Erika Beumer, who has created a website to keep the book updated and enable international communication about parenting.

A big 'Thank you' to everyone who read the early versions and contributed their invaluable opinions which have made a difference to the final copy. You gave me the confidence to carry on.

Deep thanks to my two sisters and all my friends who have walked with me through my life and have made my family so much richer - you have each been a priceless gift. This book is the product of your love, and I am grateful to each one of you.

About the author

I am a mother to six children, all now adults. I am also a retired teacher and have spent my life and career being creative and juggling work with parenting. I have never had much money but have always seen this as a springboard to better things.

For fifteen years, I have taught adults with profound learning difficulties, with no budget. I won the national BECTA (British Educational Communications and Technology) award for this work.

I have led many seminars called "Teaching on a paper bag" about how to be a better teacher with fewer ready-made resources.

In 1994, I published an autobiography under a pseudonym with Hodder and Stoughton which was translated into two other languages. This led to an extensive seminar programme spanning eight years.

I have regularly organised projects that support communities. I have a great passion for helping those struggling with budgets and recycling and I established a free clothing store which has been in operation for over twenty-five years. I currently manage a project which offers a safe space for people to enjoy.

Printed in Great Britain
by Amazon